BREAKING
BACK

BREAKING BACK

HOW I LOST EVERYTHING AND WON BACK MY LIFE

JAMES BLAKE

WITH ANDREW FRIEDMAN

HarperCollinsPublishers

HarperCollins books may be purchased for educational, business, or sales promotional use. For information please write: Special Markets Department, HarperCollins Publishers, 10 East 53rd Street, New York, NY 10022.

FIRST EDITION

Designed by Kris Tobiassen

Library of Congress Cataloging-in-Publication Data has been applied for.

ISBN 10: 0-06-134349-8
ISBN 13: 978-0-06-134349-0

07 08 09 10 11 DIX/RRD 10 9 8 7 6 5 4 3 2 1

CONTENTS

Author's note ix

Prologue 1

1. The Statement 7

2. It Could Be Worse;
   It Could Be Raining 35

3. Requiem for a Superman 63

4. Five Minutes of Hitting,
   Twenty-Five Minutes of Talking 115

5. Plan B 147

6. If You Can Win One Set,
   You Can Win Two 175

7. Fire It Up One Time . . . *Bam!* 203

8. Getting Better 241

   Epilogue 257

   Glossary 265

   Acknowledgments 269

THIS BOOK IS BECAUSE OF, AND FOR, MY FATHER, TOM.
I CAN'T EVEN IMAGINE WHERE I WOULD BE WITHOUT HIM
AND THE LESSONS HE HAS TAUGHT ME.

AUTHOR'S NOTE

If you don't play or watch tennis, I've included a short glossary of important words, terms, and information at the end. I hope these make the story equally approachable to tennis fans and not-yet-fans as well.

Thanks for reading.

PROLOGUE

During the summer and fall of 2004, I had a lot of impromptu parties in the living room of my house in Fairfield, Connecticut. The music was blaring on the stereo, beer, chicken wings, and burgers from nearby Archie Moore's restaurant on the kitchen counter, and friends from every era of my life hanging out—the fact that they had work, other friends, other lives, didn't seem to matter much. In hindsight I remember those months as one long get-together, although the gatherings took different forms: sometimes we'd all just hang and catch up, sometimes we'd watch a ball game, and sometimes we played poker.

One Tuesday in September, it was a poker night and gathered around my dining room table were a bunch of guys I'd known since high school, or earlier: Evan Paushter, my best friend and the gang's designated wise guy; Matt Daly, another old friend, his camouflage baseball cap turned backward, as it always is; J. P. Johnson; Andy Jorgensen; and my brother, Thomas, who often crashes at the house when he's in town.

The scene was typical of that summer, and even though it was a "school night," poker chips and good-natured taunts were flying across the room late into the evening. As usual, we went around and around swapping unwanted cards for new ones, while seeing and upping each other's bets until there was an Everest of chips in the center of the table. Eventually, when the mountain of chips looked ready to tumble, we called our bets and each player overturned his cards, moving clockwise around the group. There was nothing too impressive—a lot of bluffing and wishing had been going on—and we laughed as each lackluster hand was revealed.

Finally, we got to Matt, who had been sitting at the end of the circle with an impenetrable stare, not giving away a thing. With the realization that there was nobody left to fool, he couldn't contain his smile anymore, brightening like a Christmas tree as he turned over his cards—a straight flush.

We all laughed. Hard. It was such a superior hand that he had us all beat by a mile.

"Fire it up one time! *Bam!*" shouted Andy, employing our group's catchphrase, which he himself coined years ago, as Matt gathered his arms around the chips, pulling them in and arranging them into neat little stacks.

Still chuckling, I stood up to get some wings, but when I

got to my feet, I began to wobble. Hoping that nobody noticed, I surreptitiously placed my hands on the table to steady myself.

It wasn't the beer. I hadn't even had a beer. It was the zoster, a virus that grabbed me back in July and hadn't let go. A vicious illness, zoster had paralyzed the left side of my face, distorted my sense of taste and hearing, and robbed me of my equilibrium. I was so comfortable with this crowd that I often forgot about the fact that I was sick, or that my face looked droopy and mangled. But anytime I tried to stand and walk, it became hard to ignore any longer.

On this Tuesday—just like every other day when zoster ravaged my body—I didn't want them to worry, and I didn't want to let those negative thoughts into the carefree air of the night, so I steadied myself on the table and walked to the kitchen as quickly as I could, before anybody noticed that I was fighting just to stay on my feet. That unsteadiness wasn't just normal for me at that time; it was how I lived every minute of the day during that summer and fall. If I had a normal job, I probably would have been back to work by then. But I didn't have a normal job. I was a professional tennis player, and I had put my career on hold to spend the rest of the year recuperating. The only catch was that the doctors told me that it could take years to recover, and so the question of whether or not I would ever play again continuously lingered in the air.

Zoster is often triggered by stress, so it made perfect sense that it hit me that summer, a season in which I had fractured and rehabbed my neck, then lost my father to a long, painful bout with stomach cancer. To say it was a stressful time would be a tremendous understatement; it was a devastating series of events. At that point, my friends and family were my one and only saving grace. I spent most days alone, while my friends were off at work, and with the silence of my house around me, I often wondered if my life had been irrevocably altered. It was only when the nights and weekends rolled around, when my friends and I were together, that I was able to lose my worries in the comfort of their company.

During those days in 2004, and the ones that followed in early 2005, my character was challenged as never before. I was at a major crossroads, a time in which my life and my career were largely in the hands of fate, despite all the efforts I was making to get better. Things could have gone either way for me then: I could have gotten back to my pro-tennis career in a matter of months, or I could have hung up my racket for good. I could have pursued a totally different, much more conventional, life, and I probably would have been very happy to do so.

But I didn't. Instead, I worked hard and turned my life around, managing to achieve a level of success that I never could have dreamed of when I was wobbling my way through my house that summer and fall.

Play tennis long enough, you realize—much as I did—that

your relationship with the ball is your relationship with life. Strokes, strategy, and stamina will only take you so far; how well you play depends on something much more idiosyncratic and much less definable. The strangest part of 2004 was not my injuries and illness but the aftermath of them, and the fact that my greatest professional successes occurred after I had faced my most daunting personal challenges. I used to think this was ironic; now I realize that my success flows directly from having cleared those hurdles.

This is the story of my relationship with life, and how I got through those dark days, arriving on the other side with a new understanding, and a new approach to everything I do, on the court, and off.

JAMES BLAKE
Fairfield, Connecticut
December 2006

ONE

THE STATEMENT

DECEMBER 2003

Even if you are on the right track, you will get
run over if you just sit there.

—WILL ROGERS

For professional tennis players, December is an annual abyss.

The year's competition is done, and everyone on the Association of Tennis Professionals (ATP) tour scatters around the planet to relax for the only month of our sport's notoriously stingy off-season. Come January, those of us who aren't nursing injuries will flock to Australia, or one of a handful of other destinations, for the first tournaments of the New Year. From there, we will continue to travel and play on and off for the better part of the next eleven months.

Success in professional sports is a funny thing. You might say that pro athletes live with three certainties looming over them: Death, taxes, *and* retirement. In the back of your mind, you know that no matter how good you are, what you've got is either fleeting or finite—at some point it's going to end, either by choice or because your body will simply give out.

So, much as we welcome our downtime in December, we must also contend with the *what-ifs* that it brings: What if I just had the best year I'm capable of? What if this slump I'm in isn't really a slump? What if it's the beginning of the long, slow slide to oblivion? Even the best player in the world faces his own versions of this question: what if this was my last year of being number one? What if that new teenager everyone's buzzing about is even better than I am? What if I get injured next year and it all comes screeching to a halt?

For most players, these are the questions that come up every December, but for me, December 2003 was the first year that I really found myself asking them. In 1999, I left college after my sophomore year to become a professional tennis player, but it took me a few Decembers before I really came to understand the abyss that the month presents. Like many young athletes, I was having too much fun for such weighty introspection. The ATP tour is like a kind of traveling neverland, where no one forces you to grow up. So a lot of the guys are indistinguishable from overgrown adolescents—when not hitting tennis balls, or the gym, we spend our time hanging out, playing poker, watching television, mastering video games, instant messaging each other, perfecting iPod playlists, and planning the occasional practical joke.

Don't get me wrong, staying fit and honing your game are hard work, and if you do them right, they consume several hours a day. In addition, there are the other commitments—interviews, photo shoots, personal appearances, and promoting whatever tournament you find yourself in on any given week. But when you stack it up against most other "jobs," life out on the tour is basically a dream, in more ways than one. It's a dream come true, because most of us grew up idolizing professional athletes and can hardly believe we've become one ourselves, and the higher you climb, the more surreal it gets. People recognize you on the street; designers throw clothes at you on the off chance that a reporter might mention it in print; hordes of children line up outside your practice court to have you autograph tennis balls, rackets, hats, or even body parts when nothing else is available; and you spend a ridiculous amount of time on airplanes, literally living among the clouds.

In some ways, I think that the experience has been stranger for me than it has for most of my peers because I was never supposed to make my living as a jock. If most adolescent athletes have "sports parents," then I had "school parents"—a mother and father who revered education above everything else and treated it as a lifelong pursuit, not just something to occupy you until age twenty-one. On a daily basis, they demonstrated their commitment to learning by using themselves as examples. My mother, Betty, is a voracious reader and occasional writer, while my father, Tom, continued to enhance his communication skills well into his fifties by reading and by taking a vocabulary-building class.

Early on, my parents had to endure some social hardships as a mixed-race couple. My father was black and my mother white, and it wasn't always easy. One night, early in their courtship, they were dining at a restaurant and my father caught another man staring at them. "I have nice teeth, too," my father said, grinning broadly at the guy. It was a private joke between him and my mom, a reference to the way plantation owners looking to purchase a slave would sometimes ask to see his teeth. The man probably didn't understand, but my mother still laughs, a little sadly, when she recounts the story.

Despite incidents like that, my parents always maintained their belief in the essential decency of people, and they passed this faith on to me and my older brother, Thomas Jr. When I was a junior player, another kid told me he felt sorry for me because of my genealogy, predicting that I'd be hated by blacks *and* whites. I told my mother about what he said, and she replied that she didn't see why I wouldn't be loved by *both* communities, an outcome that hadn't even occurred to me before she mentioned it. And fortunately for me, what she predicted is exactly what came to pass.

Optimism of that kind was infectious, and the constant support of my parents helped me to persevere through the awkward and often ignorant comments of some of the people around me. While my interracial heritage may seem to be a tailor-made story of adversity, the adversity never really materialized in many ways because I never allowed it to overtake my worldview. My parents' inclination toward truly loving life and expecting the best from it shaped my entire outlook, helping me to believe in the inherent goodness of other people and keeping me from being sucked down into the darkness that sometimes overshadows the joy of living.

My parents' optimism also carried over into tennis, a sport they both loved. They were excellent club players, and when we were teenagers, Thomas and I excelled at it as well, with each of us opting to play for the local high school in Fairfield, Connecticut. But tennis, like every other sport that we played growing up, was just a part of our lives, not the thing that defined them. In fact, it wasn't the ATP that Thomas dreamed of; it was Harvard University, a goal he attained and which subsequently influenced me. In 1997, when I headed to Cambridge, I had every intention of returning for the next three Septembers and smiling in my cap and gown for my graduation photo in the spring of 2001.

But something funny happened in my sophomore year that took me by surprise: I became the number one college tennis player in the country. It was a hard fact to ignore and it got me, and those around me, thinking that I might have the goods to go pro. While I tried not to dwell on the idea too much, it was a hard question to keep in the back of my mind, and in the end, the temptation was too great. Despite my desire to earn a Harvard degree, I decided that the opportunity to play professional tennis was irresistible.

When I first left college, as much as anything, it was to strike while the iron was hot, to see what I might be able to accomplish as a player before I was too old to give it a shot. There was always the assumption that I would return to Harvard (I actually promised my mother that I would), or at least that my return was as likely as my remaining on the pro tour indefinitely. And so, for the first few years, it was enough that I was having a great time traveling the world, playing in front of fans, and earning a pretty good living, all while chasing the sun around the globe to play wherever it happened to be summer, or at the very least, where it was hot.

Being where I was, it was easy to adopt an aw-shucks attitude about my career. After struggling for my first two years, by the end of 2001, I had become the seventy-third-best tennis player in the world according to the computer rankings, and by the end of 2002, I had worked my way up to number twenty-eight. It was more than I had ever imagined for myself, and for the first time, I started to believe that I actually deserved to be in the same league as the guys who had been training for such glory since they were old enough to walk and hold a racket.

Right after talent, health, and conditioning, confidence is about the most important thing a tennis player can possess. It's the crucial intangible of the game. It's the thing that lets you know you can really tee off on a forehand and it will land right where you want it to. It's the thing that lets you hang in during a tough point, patiently working it until the opportunity arises for a winner. It's the thing that reassures you and tells you constantly that you deserve to be where you are.

Few people are born with a lifetime supply of confidence; for most of us it's something that ebbs and flows like the tides. To oversimplify, winning builds confidence; losing takes it away. Hard-fought victories pump it up a little faster, as do triumphs over top players. By the same token, inexplicable losses, or going down to the unknown and the unheralded, can cause confidence to plummet.

The blank month of December often exposes these fluctuations in a pro-tennis player's confidence, and while December 2002 had brought my confidence and my ranking to an all-time high, by the end of the 2003 season, it was sinking like a stone. It had been a difficult year, one in which I'd lost a number of matches I felt I could, and should, have won, often due more to my mental unraveling than to what actually transpired on the court. I was about to wrap up the season in the mid—to low-thirties, my first year-end slip since turning pro.

To be fair, being among the top thirty or so players in the world is nothing to be ashamed of, unless you're capable of doing better, and I knew I was capable of doing better. My mind kept flashing back to the moments of great promise during the two previous years, and throughout the fall of 2003, those memories continuously nagged at me. I thought often of the one tournament I had won at that point, the Legg Mason Tennis Classic in Washington, DC, just over a year earlier, in August 2002, but I didn't focus on the final. Instead, I thought about my semifinal match, in which I found myself standing on a Saturday night across the net from one of my mentors, Andre Agassi, who was well into his legendary comeback and ranked number six in the world.

The atmosphere was crackling; before he retired, *nothing* electrified a stadium full of American tennis fans in August like the sight of Andre Agassi plying his trade. I could feel the anticipation building in the air from the corridor that leads to center court, and when we walked out into the arena, and the announcer called out his name—"Ladies and gentlemen, Andre Agassi"—drawing it out like Ed McMahon introducing Johnny Carson, the place went stark-raving mad.

The crowd gave me a pretty rousing reception as well. From

the time I turned pro, I always loved that moment when you walk out on the court, your name is announced, and you wave up to the fans. Tennis is an individual sport, so being a player at some level means being an entertainer, and having that time to connect with the crowd before you turn your focus to your opponent has always been very special to me.

On this particular occasion, however, the moment was almost too much to process: I had come so close to staying in school and now here I was about to play one of the icons of the game. As we began the warm-up—tennis has a gentlemanly tradition of preparing your opponent for competition by exchanging ground strokes and feeding each other volleys and overheads—I felt like a split personality. One side of me was having an out-of-body experience; the other was firmly in touch with my body and anxiously aware of the butterflies that were inhabiting my entire stomach.

Somehow, I pulled myself together, and before long, I was in the midst of one of those nights that athletes dream of, when everything just clicked and I could do no wrong. Much of the match is a blur, the way your best performances often are, but all the way through it felt good. I cracked forehands (my dominant go-to shot) left and right, while racing all over the court. I was patient when I needed to be and strong when I needed to be. Eventually, I broke him three times in two sets, to win 6–3, 6–4 in just one hour and one minute.

That was a *big* deal in my life. When I reached the semifinals, a bunch of my friends from back home in Connecticut raced to D.C. to see the match, then stuck around for the finals, where I beat Paradorn Srichaphan from Thailand.

Your first tournament victory is a milestone, a sign that you've arrived, that you're capable of being the last one standing come Sunday night. Once you've notched that first big win, who knows how many more might follow? As it turned out, none had followed.

While this was a source of great frustration during the fall of 2003, my lone tournament win wasn't the only thing that was haunting me. Constantly, I found myself revisiting two encouraging *losses* going all the way back to 2001. One occurred when I played Australian Pat Rafter in a Masters Series event in Cincinnati during August of that year. I played Rafter close in the first set, losing it 7–9 in the tie break, only to have him run away with the second set, 6–2. As match point came and went, I felt the letdown of the loss acutely, recognizing that this turn would offer a serious blow to my fledging confidence.

Rafter was one of the most popular, likable guys on the tour, and after the match, as we shook hands at the net, he leaned in close, the zinc oxide he smeared under his eyes like war paint runny with sweat: "You could have beaten me today," he said, surprising me, "but I had the sense that maybe you didn't believe it yourself." He paused, then said, *"Now* do you believe?"

It was a remarkable statement, if for no other reason, because he perceived something about me that I wasn't even admitting to myself: I didn't really believe that I belonged out there with the best players in the world. I didn't feel like I deserved to win. But when you get that close to taking a set from a top player, then lose, your belief in yourself often disappears with the set, and that's what happened that day.

A few weeks later, I made it to the second round of the US Open and took Australian Lleyton Hewitt, the number three player in the world at that time, to five sets, before the heat and my work-in-progress conditioning failed me and I ran out of gas, throwing up on the court and cramping. It was not a pretty sight. Even less pretty was that the most memorable part of that match for most people was not my performance but an outburst from Lleyton when he accused a linesman of making calls in my favor because we shared the same skin color. "Look at him, mate," I can still hear him pleading to the chair umpire. "Look at him [indicating me], and look at *him* [indicating the linesperson], and you tell me what the similarity is."

His tirade became a cause célèbre, catapulting me into the national spotlight for the first time, but I didn't revisit that match because of the controversy; I remembered it for what my coach, Brian Barker—the unassuming, gentle soul who's been my tennis mentor since I was eleven—said to me after the match. Standing in the hallway of our hotel in Manhattan—the first quiet moment we'd had since the match's end, as prior to that every minute had been consumed by the standing-room-only press conference and the general chaos that followed in the wake of Lleyton's remark—Brian looked straight at me, and without drama or sarcasm, said, "I don't care that you lost. You keep playing matches like that and you're going to win. *A lot.*"

All that promise. All that encouragement. All those believers.

And yet, as I took stock of 2003, there was no escaping the fact that I hadn't passed many road signs to success in the fast-expiring year. Rather, I had disappointments that stuck in my throat, that I thought about at night just as much as I lingered on those positive memories from '01 and '02.

I saw myself, for example, on the court at Indian Wells, California, in March 2003, losing the final set 0–6 to Gustavo "Guga" Kuerten in the quarterfinals, and standing there dumbfounded, wondering what had happened. I had beaten Carlos Moya, who at the time was number five in the world, to get to that round, and although Kuerten, a gangly, affable, loose-limbed Brazilian, had three French Open titles to his name, he was far more accomplished on clay than he was on hard courts. In addition, he was only one spot higher than I was in the rankings, number twenty-four to my twenty-five. In other words, on paper, I was just as likely to win the match as he was.

What made that match even more frustrating was that I

had won the first set, but after he won the second set to even the match, I didn't see us as tied. In my mind he was winning, and as I was apt to do in those days, I became angry with myself for letting him back in.

That match was indicative of how things went for me in 2003; to put it simply, my mind, my character, was not in the right place to win matches. In tennis, especially men's tennis, holding serve is paramount. The serve is the shot over which a player has the most control, and because it starts each point, the server has a tremendous advantage and is expected to win the game. If you lose serve, you've been "broken," and unless you can break back by winning a game on your opponent's serve, and regain equal footing, then it's impossible to win the set. One of the most telling marks of your character on the court is whether or not you can break back, because you need to pull it off when your confidence is down and your opponent's is up.

As 2003 wound down, it became clear to me that I lacked that court character. When I would get broken, I didn't regroup properly. I didn't dig in and steel myself for a comeback, and that match against Guga was a perfect example. When he got up on me, beginning with his break of my serve in the second set, I began to press, going for too much on my shots and getting impatient. Next thing I knew it was all over. The last set was as much of a blur as my win over Agassi, only it wasn't all my winners I couldn't remember; it was all my unforced errors and squandered opportunities that came together into a highlight reel from hell.

There were other tournaments, seven of them, that went by in the blink of an eye because I traveled to some destination only to lose in the first round, pack my bags, and leave town, which is not a satisfying way to spend your time and money. In other matches that year, I was simply blown away by my opponents, sometimes by guys who ranked well below me that in hindsight I didn't take seriously enough. One of the most suicidal things you can do in tennis is to believe your ranking. You don't win matches because you're number whatever; you get to your number whatever by winning matches. Going into 2003, I knew this rationally, but I didn't know it in my gut until I was at the other end of the year, when I had learned it, over and over, the hard way.

I had begun to develop a reputation: a lot of fans, sportscasters, and journalists thought I had talent, but the prevailing feeling was that I didn't want to win badly enough. People opined that when the chips stacked against me, I'd just start flailing rather than patiently solving whatever problem was in front of me on a given day. What made matters worse was that I wore my frustration on my sleeve, shaking my head and moping around the court. To many observers, this was evidence that I had a tendency to give up on a match that wasn't going my way, an appraisal that annoyed me because, if anything, I wanted to win *too* much. I always had a feeling, deep down, that I was capable of playing great tennis, and when I didn't, I was almost mystified by it. I'd try to do something spectacular to turn things around, and almost inevitably ended up making things worse. But despite the speculation to the contrary, I was always trying, and that people doubted my heart left a bad taste in my mouth.

In the end, it really didn't matter what I thought or felt. My situation was what it was. I was at the end of 2003 without a second title, a ranking that was moving in the wrong direction, and enough regrets to last a lifetime. That year, as I flew home for Christmas, was the first time that I heard the rumblings of my personal *what-ifs*.

Because my optimistic outlook, my *what-ifs* took a positive tone: *What if,* I thought to myself, *I took my game to the next level? What if I stopped losing to guys I know I can beat? What if I didn't get down on myself when I found myself in a bad patch in a match?*

My *what-ifs* were always about how well I could play the game, not about whether or not I'd attain superstar status. Personally, I wasn't afraid of slipping into oblivion. Like most people, I happen to come from oblivion, and I was always pretty happy there, so the thought of going back didn't bother me too much.

No, my personal abyss wasn't the prospect of losing matches, or fading out of the top hundred, or being relegated to the outer courts. It was not doing as well as I knew I could. It was the idea of beating myself. It was the dread of not living up to my potential.

————

In December 2003, my parents were still living in the house where I grew up—a modest but cozy two-story home in the Stratfield section of Fairfield, Connecticut, near where the town line separates it from Bridgeport.

Back then (and today as well), I spent a lot of my non-competition time in Tampa, Florida, where I own a house. To keep my game and fitness level up, I trained at the Saddlebrook Tennis Center, working out six days a week with the conditioning guys and practicing just as often with other touring pros who live nearby, like my old college competitor Jeff Morrison and my best friend on tour, Mardy Fish. Although for all practical purposes Tampa was where I lived, Fairfield, where my family had been since I was six, was my home. And in 2003, I bought a house within walking distance from the town center, to make sure that it always stayed my home.

From the time I left for college in 1997, I've always come back to Fairfield at Christmastime. It has a sort of Anytown, USA, feel—there's a train station and a main street (the Boston Post Road), and in the spring and summer, there are signs and banners hanging across intersections or on lampposts announcing music and arts festivals and other events. During the winter holidays, there's a real sense of conviviality in the air. It's not the smallest of small towns—local shops like Fairfield Clothiers exist right alongside outposts of national chains like Banana Republic—but it has its charms: such as the old-fashioned streetlamps that dot Post Road, or the bronze statue of Mark Twain sitting on a bench reading *Huckleberry Finn* outside one of the stores, or that the population is small enough that you might run into people you know on your rounds.

December has always been extra-dear to me, because in addition to Christmas and the New Year, it brings my birthday (December 28) and my brother's birthday (December 29), the timing of which couldn't be better, since a hodgepodge of schoolmates and people I played with in junior tennis tournaments still live and work in the area. So between the actual holidays and the personal ones, it always makes for a very social few weeks, a chance to reconnect with the people and places that have meant the most to me since childhood.

But in 2003, there was another factor that made the holidays more precious than usual. Earlier that year, in June, my brother, who had become a professional tennis player at about the same time I did, and I were in England playing Wimbledon. We've always felt at home because our mother is British by birth, and so for the past two years, my parents had come over for the tournament. This time, however, my mom made the trip alone, with plans to visit relatives afterward.

I lost in the second round, and later that day, my mother took me and Thomas aside and shared some potentially grim news with us: our father had stayed behind, in part, because he said he had to have a routine hernia operation. But my mother hadn't been able to reach him by phone or e-mail in several days, and she was beginning to think he was actually in the grip of something far more serious.

We knew what she meant. A fiercely independent and strong-willed man, my father, if he were sick, would have handled it the same way he handled the rest of his life—with unwavering self-sufficiency. This would be especially true on the eve of Wimbledon and my mother's planned vacation—there was no way he'd have let himself become a distraction to me and my brother competing, or to his wife's making her annual pilgrimage home.

She returned to the States right away, and when I finally reached her on the phone it was the middle of the night. I could tell right away that something was terribly wrong because, although she did her best to hide it, she was clearly in an emotional state. I soon understood why as she confirmed all of our worst fears; my father had been diagnosed with stomach cancer, had had a gastrectomy (a fancy way of saying that his stomach had been removed), and was recuperating at the VA hospital. About a day later, my brother and I arrived there, and we were shaken by the sight of our father, whom my mother routinely called her "iron man." He was connected to all sorts of ominous machines, pumps, and monitors; there were strange noises and people taking readings from mysterious equipment. After we'd been there for a while, a doctor came in to brief us on his condition. We were heartened when she told us that he was eligible for an experimental drug that had had some small, but positive, effect on black and Asian patients. Then she shattered our expectations all over again when she told us, with sunny optimism, that he could live up to two years, the first time any of us learned that his condition was terminal.

My mother turned to my father and spoke for all of us when she said, "We'll fight this."

My family is tight, and we share an intimacy, but it's not founded on words—we have what you might call an empathic, almost telepathic, relationship; intuiting feelings and needs, but rarely discussing them. So, we didn't talk much about my father's illness that Christmas. He was holding up astoundingly well and we all wanted to enjoy the time as normally as possible, though in the back of our collective mind we knew it could be our last holiday together, before the unit would become forever incomplete.

Being in my father's presence had always made me feel safe, and somehow he was able to project that aura even though he had begun to shrink in that insidious, creeping way that cancer sufferers do. That December, he was still either going to work or working out of the home office every day—except when he had to make one of his increasingly frequent visits to Memorial Sloan-Kettering Cancer Center in New York City for tests and procedures. He also took great pride that he continued to exercise: I was with him on one of those hospital visits when the doctor, on his way out of the room, stopped and remembered to tell my father how to limit his workouts. As soon as the door closed, Dad turned to me and said, "I did more than that just yesterday."

While my mother and brother helped shape the person I am today, more than anyone, it was my father who pushed me to do my best, just as he drove himself in everything he did. "You can't control your level of talent," he would tell me in his firm, supportive voice when I was a little kid. "But you *can* control your level of effort."

That December, for obvious reasons, I thought a lot about that statement, about my father's condition, and about the upcoming year. I thought about how special it would be to reach my potential while he was still alive to see it, to fuse effort and talent together and create something that, even with his ever-expanding vocabulary, I knew he would find too beautiful for words.

————

Not long before I came home for Christmas, I was in Europe at the indoor tournaments that dominate the last months of the tennis season. Reflecting back on my year, I began to toy with the idea of doing something symbolic to mark the end of what had come before and signal to the tennis world, my opponents, and myself that I was beginning a new phase in my career.

I began to think about shaving my head.

This would be a big decision for any twenty-three-year-old, but in my case it was especially significant because a lot of fans knew me for my hair. I was a very recognizable presence on the ATP tour—not just because I was one of the very few African Americans out there, but also because I had a pretty serious network of dreadlocks protruding Medusa-style from my head. It had been in place, in some form or another, since my college days, so it was easy to spot me around the grounds of a tournament, even from a considerable distance.

While I liked having a recognizable feature, I also began to get worried that this feature was overshadowing my playing. I wanted to be known for how I played, not just how I presented myself. Growing up, I was a huge fan of basketball deity Michael Jordan, whose eye-popping, gravity-defying, championship-hoarding exploits made him, in my book, the greatest athlete of all time. I'd once heard Jordan say that in his mind, he played for the one person in the stands who had never seen him before, and how he wanted to make sure that person saw something he or she would never forget (writer Bob Greene dubbed this expectation of witnessing something otherworldly the "Jordan sideshow"), a sentiment that had also been famously uttered by baseball legend Joe DiMaggio, who once said that, "there is always some kid who may be seeing me for the first or last time. I owe him my best."

That always seemed like an ideal to strive for as an athlete, but I had to be honest with myself: A lot of fans who saw me play in 2003 probably remembered me, more than anything, as the guy with the crazy hair.

I didn't want to be known for that anymore. I wanted to be known for my tennis. And I thought shaving my head would be a real way of telling myself to put up or shut up.

When I got to Fairfield for Christmas, I couldn't lose that idea that something needed to change, but my hair was just the beginning. I found myself living a double life. I'd spend hours hanging with friends and visiting my parents' house, giving off the air that I was fine, just the same old James. But as I drove around town, thoughts of improvement consumed me. In the mornings, I'd meet my coach, Brian, at the indoor courts of the Tennis Club of Trumbull, which was located in a nearby town where Brian grew up. (It also happened that my mother worked part-time at the desk.) Each morning, upon arrival, I couldn't wait to start. I did everything with heightened intensity—serves, ground strokes, whatever. I wasn't just hitting the ball; I was hacking away all those regrets, clearing a path into the coming New Year.

The same was true of my workouts at the local gym: I stayed on the stationary bike longer than usual, pushing myself to the point of fatigue, and I squeezed an extra rep or two into each weight-lifting set. Working out can be as monotonous for a professional athlete as it can for everybody else, but not that December. I wasn't bored for a second. Every moment was imbued with purpose.

I'm a pretty self-contained individual, and for much of my life, I've followed my father's example of not burdening others with my problems. I don't do a lot of "sharing" and never really have. But at the end of 2003 there were two people that I sought out for advice about my situation. One was Brian, who from the time we began working together had instilled in me a philosophy of "getting better" as the only long-term goal worth pursuing. Brian's point of view was that if you set specific goals for yourself, like winning a Grand Slam, or being number one, and didn't attain them, then you'd be disappointed with a great result, like reaching a slam final, or being, say, number five in the world. In time, I absorbed this philosophy and really took it to heart. Throughout my career, I had made it a point not to set any specific goals, and rather than being hung up about my ranking, a particular opponent, or even the big picture of my career, I just stayed focused on getting better. If I did that, the rest would take care of itself. (The problem with the current year, of course, was that I hadn't gotten better; if anything, I was doing worse.)

While Brian was right there with me on my desire to take things to the next level, he shrugged off my thoughts about shaving my head—I think he believed that I was just messing around and wasn't really serious about such a drastic image change.

The other person I confided in was my agent, Carlos Fleming, a former tennis professional who operated out of International Management Group's (IMG) headquarters in Cleveland, Ohio. At that point, Carlos had been my agent since the moment I first turned pro, and in those four years, he'd never seen me without my hair intact. As I spoke to him and informed him about what I was contemplating, I didn't have any illusions about my look. I knew that my appearance, as much as my tennis, was what sold the agency on me in the first place, and my hair was a big part of that equation. Although Carlos had seen me play, it was, I've been told, a *USA Today* sports section cover story on me and my brother, when we were still competing for Harvard, with a huge photo of us, that really got the other suits at the agency jazzed up about us.

"I'm thinking about shaving off my hair," I told him.

He was adamant in his reply. This was, he felt, a *bad* idea. He was renegotiating my Nike contract, which was up for renewal, and also fielding interest from other possible sponsors. Besides contributing to my prominence in the tennis world, I had been signed with IMG's modeling division since 2002 (their idea, not mine), and so my hair was a moneymaker in its own right.

I discussed some other things that were on my mind with Brian and Carlos. Though we didn't believe in setting specific goals, I wanted badly to show that an American not named Courier or Agassi could succeed on the notorious red dirt of the European courts, usually considered kryptonite to most U.S. players, even legends such as McEnroe and Sampras. I also wanted to make the United States Olympic team that would travel to Greece that summer.

I shared the idea of cutting off my hair with some others, the closest I got to giving them even an inkling of what was on my mind. My brother, who had sported hair similar to mine on and off for years, was against it, mainly because he knew how long it would take to grow it back if I changed my mind. On the other hand, Laura Sposato, one of my best friends from high school, who at the time was rooming at my house in town with our other friends Sara and Caraly (pronounced "Cara Lee"), thought I should go for it.

On Christmas Day, my family gathered at my house and we exchanged presents as we always did. My father, who had noticed that I had been wearing friendship bracelets, made for me out of knitting string by a passionate tennis fan, until they were literally falling apart, handed me a jewelry box, which was highly unusual, to say the least.

I opened it and inside was a simple gold bracelet. He explained: "Your mother and I thought it would be nice for you to have a bracelet that will last forever."

I put the bracelet on and, while I didn't say this at the time, had already decided that I'd never take it off. If it would last forever, then that's how long I'd wear it.

The next day, while visiting my parents, I borrowed a set of electric hair clippers. I took them home and put them in a drawer, closer to a decision about my hair, but still not quite there yet.

Two days later, a bunch of my friends and family members joined me at Sakura Japanese restaurant in Westport to celebrate my birthday. I had a great time as we laughed our way through holiday stories and high school flashbacks, but in the back of my mind, I couldn't stop thinking about the coming tennis year. I was pumped. Physically, I felt great, my confidence was high, and I couldn't get to Australia soon enough. My first event began on January 3, just six days away.

Time was running out to make a decision about shaving my head, and while we were at dinner, suddenly inspiration struck. An old friend, Molly Henry, and her husband, Justin, were raising money for an inner-city girls' basketball team, and I had been trying to think of a way to help her out. It occurred to me that if I cut off my hair, I could auction off the dreads, along with some memorabilia, and publicize the whole thing during my interviews in Australia, where I would no doubt be asked about my new look by the media.

That was all it took. I had lots of good reasons to shave my head and no good reasons not to, at least none that I could think of at the moment. Back at the house, I made an announcement to Laura and Caraly: "I'm going to do it. I'm cutting off my hair."

I got the clippers, went into the downstairs bathroom, and began running them over my head. I could feel the dreads coming right out, and I caught them as they fell and collected them in a plastic bag.

As I was wrapping up the job, Laura and Caraly came in.

"Omigod," Caraly said, "You look so much younger."

The two of them helped me shave the hard-to-reach spots on the back of my head, then they sat me down in the foyer and took some pictures. There was that excitement in the air that comes with doing something spontaneous, of shaking things up, for better or worse. I was feeling pretty giddy, so I picked up the phone and called Carlos at his apartment in Cleveland.

"I did it," I told him, being deliberately vague—drawing out the moment with some good-natured juvenility.

"Did what?"

"I shaved my head."

There was a long pause.

"I need to call you back," he said gravely, and hung up.

I didn't hear back from him until the next day. He had his reasons, and he would later comment to a reporter that the moment I shaved myself bald, I lost about a million dollars. That's a lot of money, more than I ever thought I'd earn in tennis, let alone endorsement deals. But I had other priorities at the moment.

I was at the start of something truly new, and with everything I had on the horizon, there was plenty to be excited about. I didn't waste time thinking about endorsement deals and advertising money—instead all I could think about was my game, about going to Australia and showing the tennis world that from here on out, I was going to be a different kind of player.

Because my father was sick, it was more difficult than usual to leave Fairfield, but he wouldn't have had it any other way. We both knew that my next step was going to be a big one, and as much as he loved having me around, nothing, not even his illness, was going to stand in the way of me taking control of my future.

As I packed my bags for the coming month in Australia, I began to visualize myself on the court. I couldn't wait to get back out there. I was going to have the best year of my career. I could feel it.

TWO

IT COULD BE WORSE; IT COULD BE RAINING

JANUARY–MAY 2004

Life is just what happens to you while you're
busy making other plans.

—JOHN LENNON, "BEAUTIFUL BOY"

During the long trip down to Australia, my luggage got lost, but
I was feeling too optimistic to take it as a bad omen.

Whenever I had a moment to myself, I envisioned the tennis year that stretched out before me, starting with the Australian swing that culminated in the Australian Open. The rest of
the year was built, more or less, around the other three Grand
Slam tournaments: the French Open in Paris in the spring,
Wimbledon on the outskirts of London in the early summer,

and the US Open at the end of summer in New York City. Each has its own surface and presents its own challenges, and I looked forward to seeing how I would do at all of them, as well as the other events that make up my sport's challenges.

I was positive and focused, but I wasn't about to let my heightened sense of purpose interfere with the fun of my new look. Not having seen any of the other players since November, I walked right past them in the locker room, or walked right up to them and just stared at them, waiting for recognition to sink in (it often took a surprisingly long time).

My favorite response came from Tony Godsick, one of Carlos's colleagues at IMG, who didn't recognize me at all. It was a funny situation because my mother, who has never been especially good at remembering names and faces, always forgot Tony's name, even though she'd met him countless times. It was something that I always gave my mom a hard time about, so it was pretty funny when Tony, who had seen my new hair (or lack thereof) when I got to Australia walked right by me in the hallway by the practice-court desk during the Australian Open. I said "Hi," and he nodded reflexively, the way you would to a stranger. It was not until we passed by each other and he was farther down the hall that I heard him start to laugh.

"Sorry, James," he called out, belatedly realizing that it was me. "I just can't get used to you with a shaved head."

"That's okay, Tony. I'm just glad I can make fun of you instead of my mom from here on in."

For the most part, that's how people responded to my hair, with a laugh and a smile. And, as I hoped would be the case, when I was asked about why I had shaved my head in the first press conferences of the year, I was able to plug my friend's charity back home.

Despite the attention that my hair attracted, it felt great to finally be in Australia. After spending the holidays in the Northeastern United States, it was invigorating to touch down in Australia—where it's summer in January—and feel the hot sun on my skin, to walk around in shorts and T-shirts. For so long I had been thinking about this time, preparing myself to play tennis on a blindingly bright tennis court in front of thousands of the most passionate fans in the world, instead of being stuck on an indoor court, alone with my coach, where the echoes of our voices and the ball are the only sounds for hours.

Ever since I first started going there, I've always loved Australia. The people are friendly, the restaurants are world class, the beaches are breathtaking, and in Melbourne, where the Australian Open is played, I stay in a hotel with its own casino, so I'm never more than an elevator ride away from honoring my one major vice: poker. But more than accommodations, Australia is where the stage is set for the tennis year. This is a very personal thing for a tennis player—most of us have no idea what the others have been up to in their time off. In the strength-sapping heat of Australia, it's easy to get a bead on who has been working hard and who hasn't, and the results you post at the Australian Open mark you as a player to watch (or not) in the coming months for tennis fans and the sports media.

For so many reasons, this place was the perfect location for me to take my new resolve out for a test drive. Between my new look and my increased fitness, I felt sure that I was coming back with an extra edge that would send a message and put me ahead of a lot of the other players right out of the gate.

Just before heading to Melbourne, I had teamed with Lindsay Davenport to win the Hopman Cup, a round-robin international team tournament played in Perth, Australia, in which each round comprises a men's singles, women's singles, and mixed doubles match, beating some top players including Czech veteran Jiri Novak and Russian Marat Safin, the great tortured artist of the contemporary men's tour, a fun, funny, great-natured guy who had won the US Open in 2000 and is capable of some of the most beautiful, powerful tennis you'll ever see.

On the heels of that success, I went to Melbourne for the Australian Open. The Australian Open, like the other three Grand Slam tournaments, is two weeks long, and in order to win you have to make it through seven rounds of play, the last three of which are the quarterfinals, the semifinals, and the final.

In each match, you play the best of five sets, which can be a grueling test of your conditioning if you push (or get pushed) that far.

The 2004 tournament was no exception, and I quickly proved that this year was going to be different. I got to the fourth round of the tournament, where I lost to Safin, who went on to the final that year. But it was a performance I was quite proud of and I definitely felt like I was achieving my goal of getting better. I was feeling great about my game—I was serving big, going for my shots, and not getting down on myself. I was playing with that combination of confidence and controlled aggression that will see you through a lot of matches.

When I'm on the road, I send out an e-mail after every match. It always has the same subject line, "results," and it goes to old and new friends in Fairfield and elsewhere, relaying the score of the match along with my feelings about it. Started sometime around 2001, the "Results Page" (as we call it) has become a real lifeline for me, in an unusual, but literal, sense of the word: it's my line back to my life. More often than not, the e-mail serves as a catalyst, prompting all my friends to start hitting "reply all" and catching up, or teasing each other, for hours.

In those first weeks of the New Year, my results e-mails were more positive than they had been in a very long time.

After Australia, I traveled back to the States, where I made it to the quarterfinals of two hard-court tournaments (the

Pacific Life Open in Indian Wells, California, and the Franklin Templeton Classic in Scottsdale, Arizona), and of the US Men's Clay Court Championships in Houston, Texas.

There were only two real disappointments for me that winter. One was that Davis Cup team captain Patrick McEnroe passed me over for a spot on the team in its tie (Davis Cup-speak for weekend-long competition) against Austria. The Davis Cup is an international competition that involves a week of practice and a three-day weekend of matches up to four times a year for as long as your nation's team keeps winning. The tie that McEnroe passed me over for was going to be played at the Mohegan Sun resort in Uncasville, Connecticut. In those days, there wasn't an ATP tournament in Connecticut, so I was excited at the prospect of being able to play in front of my friends that close to home.

The other problem was that I still hadn't won a second title, but I didn't let myself get down about the situation. I was consistently making it deep into tournaments and almost never being blown away by other players—those love sets that made little cameos in my score lines in 2003 had been eradicated. I felt like something big was just around the corner.

In April, I headed overseas, playing a tournament in Munich, Germany, before traveling to Rome to play in a Masters Series tournament (the most prestigious events after the Grand Slams) there. In the days leading up to the tournament in Rome,

I felt comfortable, but I endured a minor setback when I lost my first-round match to Jiri Novak, whom I had beaten for the first time in Australia just a few months back. It wasn't a great score line, 6–2, 3–6, 1–6, and what really bothered me was that I came apart down the homestretch, just as I had against Kuerten the previous spring. I won the first set, then lost the second. Rather than staying focused on the task at hand, playing one point at a time with patience and smarts, I got down on myself, becoming consumed by that drowning feeling I would sometimes get when a match was slipping away.

It felt like what I imagine an addiction feels like: you know you're engaging in self-destructive behavior, but you're almost powerless to stop it, and the more you continue to do it, the more pressure you feel to stop. It's a vicious cycle that can quickly become self-sustaining and cause your game to unravel.

In other words, it was exactly the kind of match I was trying not to play anymore, and I was thoroughly bummed out. About an hour later, I was hanging out in the locker room with Robby Ginepri, one of my best friends on the tour, a Georgian whose dry sense of humor can sneak up on you, thanks to his deceptively sleepy voice. Robby had just lost on the court right next to mine, and we were sitting there licking our wounds when a representative of the ATP popped in and asked us if we'd like to meet the pope; they'd been invited by the Vatican to have some players come by for a private audience the next day.

How could we resist? We decided to stick around for a while.

That night, I engaged in a James Blake tradition: barely sleeping after a loss. It's not a pretty sight. Rather than turn in, I watched CNN until the same stories began to come around again and again, I answered e-mails, sent out the Results Page ("I sucked today . . . totally forgot how to play tennis," I wrote), and played online poker until, bleary-eyed and practically sleepwalking, I finally dropped down on the bed and passed out.

In the silver-lining department, I shook off the disappointment faster than I used to. Whereas a couple of months earlier it would have taken me days to get over it, by the next morning I felt better. I knew that in the coming weeks I'd have my shots in a tournament in Hamburg and at the French Open in Paris, and I had every confidence I would do well at them.

The following afternoon, as promised, we were escorted by a Vatican security detail to meet the pope following an outdoor Mass at the Vatican. As if that weren't enough of a thrill, that night I was invited to a party hosted by Giorgio Armani himself—his collections of the past twenty years were displayed in a huge warehouse-type facility that had been transformed into an event space for the evening. Among the hundreds of people who strolled the floor to the flashing lights and pulsating music were models whom I didn't know by name but instantly recognized from magazine covers.

Like I said before: life out on the tour is often one long dream.

The next day, an overcast Thursday, I played a practice set with Robby on an outdoor clay court, at a park away from the tournament grounds. Clay, which is a notoriously difficult surface for most American players, takes some getting used to, and with the French Open only a few weeks away, I needed every day of practice. It was a casual afternoon: me, Robby, Brian, and Robby's friend John Thompson, a teaching pro who travels with Robby when his coach, Francisco Montana, can't make it. A practice set is different from actual competition in a lot of ways: First, there's obviously less pressure. Second, there can often be quite a bit of talking. As of right now, there's no coaching permitted in tennis, although some tournaments are experimenting with it (for the record, I'm all for it), but in a practice set, your coach can pipe right in and tell you what you should've done on the previous point. Brian's a very cautious and private guy, but even he will chime in now and then in this kind of setting. There's also a fair amount of good-natured trash talk.

We sometimes place a bet on practice sets, though it's not often monetary. This particular set was a "butt's-up" set, meaning that the loser stands on the baseline on one side of the court, back to the net, and bent over like he's touching his toes, so his butt is up in the air. The other player stands at the opposite baseline and fires a serve at him. It's not the same stakes as getting through to the next round of a tournament, and the prize money that comes with it, but it's a pretty good incentive not to lose, especially when you're playing against someone like Andy Roddick, another American on the tour whose serve has been clocked at over 150 miles per hour.

As it began to drizzle, we briefly halted our play, then took back to the court when it stopped. As tennis fans know, clay is unique among surfaces because after it rains, you don't need to wait for it to dry—unlike grass, which has to be covered with a tarp, or hard courts, which need to be tended to with towels, squeegees, and blowers, clay courts can be played damp because they simply absorb the moisture.

At least that's the conventional wisdom.

We returned to the court and before too long, Robby was on the verge of winning. He had a set point, and as we played out what could have been the final point, we moved each other side to side across the court. After we traded several ground strokes, he finally made as if he was going to drive a backhand, but at the last second, he carved under the ball and sent a drop shot drifting my way.

Anyone who knows me knows that I *hate* being drop shotted, even in a practice set. (My Davis Cup teammates love trying to get away with it in our practice sessions, to the point that it's become a bit of an in-joke.) I took off running full throttle at the net, my racket outstretched before me, ready to flick the ball back over to his side.

As I raced for it, the ball hit the net cord, rolled over to my side of the court, and bounced right on the sideline. I began to slide toward the ball, but my feet caught in the damp clay, and *then* on the edge of the sideline. Suddenly I was airborne, propelled headfirst toward the steel net post.

I instinctively turned my head . . .

. . . and rammed the post with my neck. I don't remember exactly what transpired over the following few seconds, but the next thing I knew I was on the ground in a heap.

We all know that our fortunes can change in the blink of an eye, and while this truth is an abstract one, we tend to think of it in somewhat predictable particulars—a plane crash, a car accident, a terrorist attack. The last thing I expected when I stepped out onto the court that afternoon was even the *possibility* of catastrophe, but there I was lying on the court with no idea of what to do next.

I wanted to do a quick analysis of the situation, but my mind was whirring much too quickly. I was strangely disconnected from the world around me, in a place beyond pain and discomfort. I hadn't quite blacked out, but my eyes were closed and the darkness was comforting, transporting. Deep down, almost subconsciously, I was aware that I had just suffered a serious injury, and that once I opened my eyes, there was a terrible reality to be confronted. So I lingered in the darkness, putting off the inevitable for just a few seconds.

Gradually, I became aware of voices talking to me.

"Are you okay?"

"James?"

"You all right?"

My lungs, diaphragm, and every other organ that helps you breathe seemed to be shut down, or stalled.

"It's . . . hard . . . to . . . breathe," I managed to say, then began gasping for air all over again.

I felt several sets of hands on my body, and refocused on the here and now, synching back up with my physical self. Until then, I hadn't realized that I had been lying on my stomach, but in one swift and controlled move, the hands turned me over onto my back. I opened my eyes, and looking straight up, there was nothing above me but sky. The dark gray of the rain clouds seemed like they were about to dissipate, gently drifting apart and making way for a late-afternoon burst of sun.

A face leaned into view. It was Brian, and he was positively freaked out. Suddenly, it all came back: I was in Rome. I was on a public tennis court. And I had just crashed, headfirst, into a steel net post.

I continued to reenter my body, and I began to feel pain in the back of my neck—closing my eyes, I pictured the vertebrae there, and I imagined bright, pulsating light radiating from the uppermost discs. I felt a dull pain all the way around my neck, and it was getting worse by the second.

The thoughts came even faster now, a moment of panic brought on by the claustrophobic lack of air in my lungs, my eyes darting around for answers. Quick little images whizzed through my brain, one right after the other—I imagined getting up, shaken but stable; I imagined myself on an operating table; I imagined myself in a wheelchair.

Robby and John leaned into view.

"Where are you hurt?" asked Brian.

"My neck hurts pretty badly," I said, then gasped. Not at the realization, but because I still had an urgent need for oxygen, made worse every time I tried to talk.

Brian took off running to call for an ambulance, while Robby and John began to grab my hands and feet, asking if I could feel them. Thankfully, I could.

By then, it was late in the afternoon, and the air was starting to cool down. As if that wasn't bad enough, the rain, which just minutes ago looked as if it had finished for the day, returned. (Even though I was sprawled out and motionless on the tennis court, I couldn't help thinking of that line in *Young Frankenstein* where the two guys are digging in a graveyard at night and one says to the other, "It could be worse; it could be raining," at which point the skies open up.) Rather than risk moving me under cover, Robby and John covered me with towels, dry clothes, and anything else they could find in their bags.

"Don't move, man."

"It's gonna be okay. Just hold still."

Listening to their possibly empty reassurances, I felt like a guy from a war movie who is about to expire, but all his buddies comfort him by whitewashing the grim reality. Was I getting a sugarcoated version of the situation? Who knew? And, besides, I was mute for the moment, too depleted to say anything more. Lying there, with the damp clay beneath my back and the falling rain covering my entire body, I gave myself over to the cooling sweat on my body that was slowly leaving me in a cold stupor.

––––––––––

It was somehow fitting that, if I was going to have an accident of this magnitude, I would have it on a tennis court, because much of my life has played out on a tennis court, including the courtship that brought me into this world in the first place.

My parents met playing tennis. My mom, a native of Oxfordshire, England, who moved to the States when she was sixteen, played as a little girl, then took it up socially at Fay Park in Yonkers, New York. It was there that she met my father, Thomas Blake, who had been introduced to tennis in the air force. While stationed in Turkey in 1966, a friend named Ray Pitts made him a deal: "You teach me basketball; I'll teach you tennis."

My brother, Thomas Jr., was born in 1976. I followed in 1979, and when I was born, my parents were still living in Yonkers. I don't remember much about the area, but it wasn't the safest of neighborhoods. My father carried a big stick with him as a precautionary measure when he walked the dog, and our house was burgled three times during the years that my parents lived there. At the time, I also didn't really understand why my father never let my brother or me walk behind him on the street. As a toddler, I thought it was a game, but when I got older, I understood that he wanted to have us in his sights at all times. But in spite of these problems, the realities of our surroundings never really registered to me, perhaps because our house was such an oasis of beauty and charm, a tasteful two-story residence with pillars outside and outdoor balconies all over the place. My parents, especially my father, exuded an aura of safety, so much so that although they enforced a number of security-motivated rules, like not allowing me to venture outside by myself, I never perceived the lawlessness around us.

My parents kept playing tennis even when my brother and I were too young to really play ourselves. Rather than entrust us to a sitter, they'd bring us along to the park, where we'd do all kinds of things to amuse ourselves, from playing stickball in an adjacent concrete lot to pushing each other on the swings to climbing on the jungle gym, or on whatever nearby structure we could find a way up. But our favorite thing to do was to pick up anything—a rock, a discarded soda can, whatever—and hit it with a stick. We could do that forever. One day, one of the friends my mom was hitting with came up to me and asked if I would just pick up anything and hit it.

"Anything but doody," I told him. (My mother still thinks that's hilarious to this day.)

When my parents were done playing, my mom would take me out on the court and feed me balls—I was much too young to have any idea about the intricacies of the game, and much too small to hit the ball with anything resembling a proper stroke. I had a two-handed backhand in those days, and a two-handed forehand as well, because I needed both hands just to pick up and swing the racket. The only goal was to get the ball over the net and keep it inside the lines on the other side—according to her, I *never* missed; whether that's the unvarnished truth or a proud mom's embellished recollection, I'll never know. (Actually, my mom says that my fascination with tennis started even earlier, before I could walk, when I'd unscrew the pole from a wooden Fisher Price vacuum cleaner toy and hit tennis balls across the kitchen floor with it, then crawl over, retrieve them, and hit them again.)

When I was six, my parents moved to Fairfield, Connecticut, where I had an active suburban childhood—my friends and I were always outside in the spring and summer, playing whatever we felt like in those days: in addition to tennis, baseball and basketball were popular in our crowd. It was a far cry from Yonkers; instead of having to hold my brother's hand to cross the street, the street was now the place where we played.

But fun was always balanced by discipline, even when we were little. My father was a paragon of self-control, self-improvement, and self-actualization—he could set his mind to any goal and then methodically take the steps to achieve it, whether it was long-term health or short-term pleasure. Though he had been a social drinker and a smoker earlier in his life, he had given those up and become devoutly vegetarian, fasting every Wednesday and exercising every morning—no matter what. If his work took him out of the house at 6:00 AM, you could be sure that at 5:00 AM, he'd be up doing sit-ups and push-ups, and lifting weights.

When he decided to take up golf in his early forties, Dad attacked it with the same intensity, reading instructional books and studying the masters when they played on television. He got down to a fourteen or fifteen handicap pretty quickly, and eventually he was down to about a ten. He probably would have improved even more, but he had a lot of things competing for his time, namely his job and his devotion to me and my brother, whom he drove around to tennis practice, tournaments, and anywhere else we needed to be.

My parents insisted on instilling the same discipline in me and Thomas, nudging us to read by rewarding us with a twenty-five-dollar prize for every hundred books completed, the titles recorded on lists that my mother still keeps to this day. As an adult, when I would call home from tournaments, my father's first question was always, "What are you reading?"

Lying on that court in Rome, I thought about how a few weeks earlier I had answered that question with a response that now seemed prophetic. I had recently finished *Rise and Walk,* the story of New York Jets defensive end Dennis Byrd and how he literally got back on his feet after having been paralyzed in a freak accident on the football field.

––––––––

About half an hour after the accident, the ambulance arrived. A team of paramedics scurried onto the court, performed a triage-type exam, fitted a neck brace around me, and loaded me onto a stretcher whose halves snapped together under me. As they carted me away, Robby employed some vintage gallows humor, yelling out, "Okay, James, see you later on for dinner."

He couldn't see it, but I smiled big at that one.

I expected that I'd be rushed off to a private hospital, but Italian protocol—as it was explained to me, anyway—dictated that all patients must first be seen at a public facility. So, with Brian seated beside me in the back of the ambulance, I was whisked to a hospital that did *not* inspire confidence. Ancient buildings are one of the charms of a city like Rome, but not when you're in need of urgent medical care and you pull up to a place that looks as old as the Coliseum.

Once inside, Brian and I were separated. He was confined to the waiting room while I was wheeled away on a gurney and abandoned in some kind of holding area. Although my disorientation had passed, I recognized that I was in completely uncharted territory. Everybody around me was, naturally, speaking Italian, and I had no idea what to do or what was being done. Would I simply lie there for hours, or would I be seen in a matter of minutes? Could I get up and go to the bathroom, or would that threaten my fragile condition?

Oh yeah, and I had something else on my mind, though I was doing my best to keep it at bay: would I ever be able to play tennis again?

Finally, I was wheeled into a lab where a technician took what felt like an endless series of X-rays—at least fifteen, maybe more—of my neck and back. He then carted me off to a private room where I was joined by Brian, whose familiar face was an enormous comfort. The technician moved me onto an examination table and tried to evaluate my condition, or so I assumed, by taking my arms in his hands and attempting to pull me up to a sitting position. He got me about halfway there when the pain in my back became unbearable, and I asked him to lower me back down.

Before he left, he matter-of-factly told me that I should be okay in about a month or two, and Brain looked at me the same way he did from the player's box when I win a match, like we could conquer the world together. Two months for an injury isn't bad at all; for a broken neck, it seemed almost like a total reprieve.

A few minutes later, another doctor, this one a bit older, came in wearing a white lab coat. In his hands, he held the black and white X-rays, still slick with darkroom fluid. He slapped them up on a wall-mounted light box, and spoke to me in English that was broken, at best.

"You have *solosis*," he said.

"Pardon?"

"*Solosis.*"

I looked at Brian and then he and I looked at the doctor together, clueless as to what he meant.

The doctor reached up around his neck and patted himself on the back.

"*Solosis.* The spine, it curves."

"Oh, right," I said. "*Scoliosis.* Yes. I've had it since I was thirteen."

He showed the X-ray to me: "It makes it hard to see." He went on to explain that I definitely had a fractured vertebra in my neck, but that he couldn't tell if I had also fractured one in my back, along the curve.

"But I'll be okay in about two months, right?" I asked, echoing what I'd just been told by the technician.

"No no no," he said: "One year. This take one year."

This was all too much to bear—the conflicting conclusions, that they were being delivered in a hard-to-understand facsimile of English, that I didn't know any of these doctors, and so couldn't decide whom to believe or trust.

With the help of the ATP, arrangements were made to have me transferred to a private hospital, a more intimate, modern boutique-type operation where more tests were performed, namely a computerized axial tomography scan (commonly called a CAT or CT scan) and further X-rays.

As I had time between doctor visits and hospital transfers, I made some necessary phone calls back home. I didn't want to tell my parents about the accident, but I had to let them know before they read it somewhere, so I did what my father would have done in the same situation, minimizing the information to cause the smallest amount of concern. I told *everyone* as little as possible—in the voice mail I left my housemate Laura, I framed it as a mere FYI to her, Caraly, and Sara, telling them I had an injury and was coming back to the house soon, but not divulging any further details.

Once I was settled at the new hospital, a middle-aged doctor, who spoke much better English than my previous physicians, told me that I had not fractured a vertebra in my back, just the one in my neck. (I later learned that the pain I felt when the technician pulled on my arms was what's known as "referred pain"; though the injury was in my neck, the network of nerves caused me to perceive it farther down as well.) The doctor was optimistic, but told me that I should stay in the hospital, try to remain as still as possible, and that he would see me again on Sunday, when he would perform an MRI (magnetic resonance imaging) for a better look.

I was miserable. Because they had snapped a neck brace on me at the scene of the accident, I was still in the clothes I'd been wearing when Robby and I were slugging it out on the court. The smell of dried sweat and clay were fermenting into a sour stench that worsened by the hour, masked only by the sweatpants I had pulled on over my shorts. As if the smell weren't enough, I was immobile, and my considerable pain was unmasked by medicine. Growing up, my parents had taught my brother and me to not take pain relievers—my mother believed they were terrible for your stomach—but over the years, I had come to like the comfort of knowing what was going on with my body at all times. So even though the pain was more intense than any I'd ever known, I kept this counsel even under these circumstances.

This whole combination of irritants was irking me. After the doctor left, I became even more annoyed because it had occurred to me that he was one of the tournament medics and was putting me off so he could spend the weekend watching the semifinals and finals rather than expediting my discharge. It was a frustrating reality to face, and one that soured my already bleak mood.

The only silver lining was that Brian was there with me. He was parked in the armchair beside my bed and clearly wasn't going anywhere.

Later that evening, Brian leaned in close to me.

"You know something," he said. "On the one hand, looking at you lying here, it makes me want to cry."

I had no idea what "the other hand" could possibly be, so I just listened.

"On the other hand, I have to say, there's something kind of funny about this."

Funny? OK, I thought, *just keep listening.*

Brian continued: "I mean, you're a professional tennis player. You were playing a *practice* set that didn't even matter."

I began to smile, realizing where he was going with this.

"You run after a drop shot. And you trip."

The smile widened.

"And break your neck."

Maximum smile.

"I mean, at some point, down the line, we're going to laugh at this."

"Yeah, Brian," I said. "We definitely have to laugh."

He kept going: "I mean, I'm your coach, and I okayed the court!"

I cracked up. The jostling of my body sent shooting pain up my spine. But it was worth it.

Brain turned serious: "You know, James, no matter what happens from today on out, you've really done great."

I just listened.

"You have so much to be proud of, and whatever happens you've got so many people around you who love you and care about you. You'll be fine."

What could I say? He was right. I remembered something that Arthur Ashe once said of how he coped with being diagnosed with HIV, the result of a tainted blood transfusion: "If I were to say 'God, why me?' about the bad things, then I should have said 'God, why me?' about the good things that happened in my life." I decided right then and there to put away whatever self-pity might have been taking shape and instead resolved to deal with the consequences of the accident as positively as possible.

It's almost unheard of for a professional tennis player to have the same coach from age eleven into the prime of his touring years, but to me it's always seemed like the most natural thing in the world. When I first got out on the tour, people would pull me aside in locker rooms and corridors, look around furtively to make sure no one was listening, and whisper into my ear that I should drop this Barker guy from back home and find a more seasoned touring coach. The advice almost never came from truly objective observers; it always seemed to be from people who had something to gain from the decision, usually coaches who were interested in taking me on themselves.

In spite of these repeated suggestions, I never considered dropping Brian because I've always known two things about him: one, that he's a great coach, and, two, that he's the best possible coach *for me*. Brian gets me. He knows when to push me and when to lie low; what I need to hear to feel good, and what will send me into a spiral of pessimism. He also knows my game—not just my strengths and weaknesses, but my inclinations, frustrations, and desires—as though it were his own.

That he knew how to make me laugh when I had a fractured neck and smelled worse than a sewer rat didn't hurt matters either.

I had never felt so good about having Brian as my coach as I did laid up in that hospital room, with him beside me, acting more like an older brother than a guy on the payroll. Would another coach, one with whom I had a strictly professional relationship, have done that, or would he have been on his way home, quietly planning the vacation he'd take while I was recuperating?

But having Brian there made me realize that I needed other people with me as well, not that I'd *ever* ask any of them to interrupt their lives to fly across an ocean to be with me. I thought about my father and how he'd sent my brother, my mother, and me off to England not even a year prior, knowing that he'd be wheeled into an operating room within days, and choosing to face that mortal struggle alone rather than come between us and our plans. After his example, how could I impose on him, or anyone, by asking them to come to me to hold my hand in my dark hour?

However, I did crave his company, and that of my family and friends back home. I knew I could get through whatever this injury had in store for me, but I had to do it in Fairfield. I couldn't do it this far away. So I decided to do what I thought my father would have done in the same situation.

"Hey, Bri," I said.

"Yeah."

"We're leaving here tomorrow."

"We can't. You heard what the doctor said. They need to run some—"

Brian also often acts as my human reality check, pointing out when something I have in mind is outlandish or simply a bad idea. I usually welcome his input because it comes from the heart, and he's often correct. But on this particular day I didn't want to hear it. I cut off my mentor, my friend, and spoke to him in a way I never had before: "We're leaving. Tomorrow. Tell them. Get us a flight and a car and get me out of here."

I don't know what he told the doctors, but Brian made the necessary arrangements.

The only bright spot during that day was that the hospital staff permitted me to take a quick shower, on the condition that I keep my neck as still as possible. I could've stayed under that hot water for an hour, but I was in and out in about three minutes. I was so dirt-caked that the water felt grainy as it ran between my toes and down the drain.

The next day, it was time to go. No one at the hospital thought that my decision to leave was a good idea—in fact, the tournament doctor had made an impassioned plea for me to reconsider—but, in truth, there was little they could do to keep me there. With a skeptical nurse watching, I got up into a sitting position and gingerly swung my legs out over the edge of the bed. I slid down to a hunched-over standing position and gradually straightened up. The impact of individual steps sent a current of pain up and down my spine, and so I was forced to shuffle gingerly out of the room and down the corridor, sticking close to the walls in case I lost my balance.

Brian followed close behind me, and when we got outside I crouched down and somehow got into the backseat of the waiting car. Brian got in on the other side, slammed the door shut, and we headed to the airport. An attendant with a wheelchair met us there and got us to the plane, where they had given us the front-most seats in first class so that I wouldn't have to contend with navigating the narrow aisles or with questions or stares from any tennis fans who might be aboard.

The flight from Rome to New York is about six hours long, but it felt much, much longer. After the shock of the injury, the chaos of the hospitals, the flurry of contradictory diagnoses, and my insistent departure for the airport, it was the first extended time I had to really be alone with the possible repercussions of what had happened.

I thought about my career and about how much effort I'd put into taking it to the next level, and I wondered if, ironically, my last match would be that frustrating loss of a few days earlier. I thought about how quickly and randomly the accident was— there are two net posts on every tennis court in the world, and I'd never heard of anyone ramming headfirst into one. I also worried about my mother, about managing her reaction to my condition, and about all my friends back in Fairfield, whom I desperately needed to see and to be with, but whom I also didn't want to inconvenience with my injury or my presence.

The neck brace kept me from feeling too much pain, even during the occasional burst of turbulence, but I was so worried about aggravating my injury that I didn't drink more than an occasional mouth-moistening sip of water on the flight for fear that I'd have to go to the bathroom. I just sat there, alone with my thoughts, patiently, stubbornly rocketing my way back home.

THREE

REQUIEM FOR A SUPERMAN

MAY–JULY 2004

Think of him still as the same, I say;
He is not dead—he is just—away!

—JAMES WHITCOMB RILEY, "AWAY"

When I was a little kid, and even when I grew up to be a young man, my father was like Superman to me. He wasn't a crime fighter, and he didn't wear a cape. In fact, in his everyday life, as a salesman of medical equipment and supplies for the 3M corporation, he lived a more mild-mannered existence than Clark Kent ever did, shuttling between the regional office and making sales calls to hospitals in New York and New Jersey. When he walked out the front door in his suit and tie each morning, briefcase in hand, got in his car, and disappeared down the street, he looked like any other businessman off to a day of work.

While there are many adults who in retrospect say that their parents seemed to possess superhero qualities, his were something that my brother and I recognized when we were growing up. He towered over us, like a figure imbued with otherworldly powers, no less extraordinary to us than any caped crusader in any comic book or film. One of the reasons we regarded our father this way was that, as far as any of us knew, he had never been sick a day in his life. He certainly *never* missed a day of work. A former military man, he embraced a life of discipline and reaped the benefits—after his early-morning calisthenics and a full day of work, it was typical for him to play a round of golf or a game of tennis before coming home and joining the family for dinner. His was a structured world, but one in which he controlled the structure, allowing him to be the guardian of his routine.

My father never talked about his own problems, though I'm sure he had them. Brian often tells about the year he and my parents shepherded me to the USTA (United States Tennis Association) National Tennis Championship in Kalamazoo, Michigan. He and my father, who had become friends by that point, sneaked off to play a round of golf one morning, after which Brian asked my father if he'd like to get something to eat.

"Can't do it," my father said. "It's Wednesday."

"So?" asked Brian.

"I fast on Wednesday."

In all the time that he had known Brian, which at that point was about five years, my father had never told him that he fasted once a week. It was just something that he did but didn't feel the need to boast about. It was typical of him. He played his cards close, not by design but by habit. If people really wanted to find out, eventually they would.

But while he was notoriously tight-lipped about his own life, one of his greatest joys was learning about others. Every night at dinnertime, he would bound through the door, without a trace of stress, asking each one of us how our day had been. Often he could barely contain his excitement. Dinner was the first time that he had seen all three of us since the morning, and he would be overflowing with questions, quizzing us on every aspect of our day (including those that we weren't always excited to share).

Not only did he listen to daily summaries from my mother, my brother, and me, but his interest in strangers was legendary among friends and family. Later during that same week at Kalamazoo, my father got to talking to a young couple who were there to watch tennis while he was sitting in the bleachers where the matches were played. When Brian found him sitting there, my father introduced him to his new acquaintances, giving a quick biographical sketch of each.

After they left, Brian turned to my father, struck that the couple hadn't wished him good luck. "Thomas," he said, "did you ever mention to them that your son is playing in the finals of the tournament?"

"No," my father replied, matter-of-factly. "They never asked."

At home, my parents had distinctly different personalities, with my mother being an incredible softie, tolerant of even the most sophomoric behavior. Years earlier, when my friends and I were young kids competing at the junior level, and my tennis-playing friends would spot my mother at a tournament, they'd lovingly mock her, calling out to her from great distances, in high-pitched, faux-British accents: "Betty! Betty Blake!" (I guess we haven't grown up too much, because they still do this once in a while when they come to see me play, even at the US Open.) And when she was the designated driver to a weekend tournament, we'd embarrass her without mercy. My best friend, Evan Paushter, who has always been the resident jester of our group, and I were especially relentless, throwing tennis balls at passing cars on the highway, making signs to embarrass other drivers, and generally acting pretty obnoxiously. Looking back, it's pretty shocking that she put up with as much as she did, but for some reason, she did.

My father, on the other hand, was Mister Serious. Road-tripping with him was all business. We'd sit in the car, hands in our laps, faces forward, talking at a respectable level and not even considering getting out of line. At matches, the situation was the same. If I threw a tantrum during a match, I'd have to answer to him after the handshake, and those were the rare times he'd get really pissed at me. If my behavior was bad enough, he might even let me have it right there, in front of the other players and parents. The reality was that during those matches and that time of my life, I needed to learn how to keep my anger and frustration in check. When my father chewed me out on the car ride home or in front of the other players, he was doing it to help me gain control over my temper. It didn't make the situation any easier to listen to (when he wanted to he had this large booming voice that could make a whole room vibrate), especially since I knew that he was right.

Dad was drill-sergeant strict, and he expected me and Thomas to behave responsibly at all times, not just on the tennis court. He even set rules to help keep us out of trouble, like the curfew he imposed on us well into our teen years, a holdover from his own experiences with racism. On Friday and Saturday nights, my brother and I were often the only black kids in our group, and my father was fearful that should we ever be pulled over by the police, we'd be singled out, partially because he'd been harassed for no good reason earlier in his own life. So, he was especially angry on the night when a bunch of my friends and I decided to have some fun by throwing eggs at passing cars from a golf course. A patrol car discovered us and we were brought in to the local station. The other kids were all older than

I was, so they just had to pay a fine, but because of my status as a minor, the police told me that I was getting off easy: no fine, just a call to my parents.

When they told me this, I almost wet my pants imagining how angry my father would be. Not only had I been acting like an idiot, but I had been doing it at night in a predominantly white section of town. I was courting the very trouble that he'd always gone to great lengths to help me avoid, and I'd gotten caught.

"Please don't call my father," I begged the sergeant on duty. "I'll pay the four hundred dollars." Then, remembering that I didn't have four hundred dollars to spare, I offered to work off the money.

They wouldn't have any of it. They called my father and he picked me up at the police station. When he arrived, he was as jovial as ever, thanking the officers for their trouble and wishing them all a good night. But I knew what was coming, and sure enough, as soon as we were both in the car and he slammed his door shut, he unleashed a diatribe so deafening it was a miracle the windshield didn't shatter.

It was harsh, but as always, I knew I deserved it. More important though, it achieved the desired effect: I never did anything like that again.

He also provided me with the perfect role model of how to be a good husband when the time comes. He and my mother were something of an odd couple—not only because he was black and she was white, but also because his New Yorker's directness and her British sense of decorum were so opposite. But they were so devoted to each other's happiness that they sometimes barely got out of the house on a "date night" because each insisted on knowing what the *other* one wanted to do, leading to dialogues that went on endlessly.

For all of the perks that come with it, I've never been especially taken with fame, and the reason is my father. To me, it's almost absurd that people regard me as a celebrity, but my father wasn't known outside of his company or his community. As I got older, I gradually got to know my father as his friends knew him, but I didn't realize until I became an adult how much work it took to maintain his level of fitness. Before he got sick, he was still a vital and imposing man with huge muscles, a straight back, and legs as strong as tree trunks. He had these enormous demonstrative hands, hands that came to life when he spoke, and even more so when he worked. They were strong hands, reassuring hands that made you feel safer the instant they touched your shoulders.

———

When our plane touched down at JFK Airport in New York, I summoned all of my father's examples and resolved to be as little of a burden, or concern, as he had been with his illness. I had been wheeled to the plane in Rome, but I walked from the plane at JFK because I knew my mother would be beside herself if she saw me in a wheelchair. Taking long strides sent pain up and down my spine, so I did a sort of shuffle along the carpeted floor of the concourse, which made for a long, slow slog out of the terminal.

Brian walked beside me, both of our carry-on bags slung over his shoulder, keeping to my snail's pace. As we trudged along, I noticed—more than I usually did—elderly passengers making their way to and from flights. In big groups and small groups they hobbled through the terminals, some of them moving gingerly about while others persevered with steadfast determination to keep moving, to keep going. And there I was right beside them, half a century younger and matching them stride for stride. I was walking more like a senior citizen than a twenty-four-year-old, only my movements weren't impeded by age, arthritis, or other ailments, and time hadn't forced me to use a cane or a walker. Suddenly everything that had seemed vitally important three days earlier no longer was.

I laughed.

"What's so funny?" asked Brian.

"I'm just wondering if this is what it feels like to be old," I said.

We didn't say anything else, but the thought lingered in

my mind. I'd never really considered what it would feel like to age, to feel your body grow infirm beneath your skin. Athletes spend a great deal of time focused on their bodies and attuned to their changes, but as I walked, I found it hard to think beyond the immediate, to speculate how my body would respond to what life had in store for it now that this curveball was thrown my way.

The thought kept growing, feeding on itself, expanding almost faster than I could keep up with it: I was only twenty-four, but how could it be that I'd never thought about this? I'd been living my life as though I'd be young forever. Given my surroundings, it was easy enough to understand why, but still I never questioned it. I had spent the past several years doing little more than working out and playing tennis or poker, often in front of enormous crowds. A few days ago I was kissing the pope's ring and hanging out at a Giorgio Armani party. And that was after *losing* a match.

I had worked hard—incredibly hard—to get where I was, but the truth was that I was living a rare and precious existence, but until I was shuffling along through that airport terminal, I had never stopped to think of it in those terms. In just fifteen years I'd be nearly forty, well on my way to middle age, with the peak of my career behind me, if the whole thing wasn't already over. I thought, too, of athletes who had been taken down or hampered by injury. One of my mentors, Andre Agassi, then just thirty-four, was struggling with a chronic back condition, and another, Todd Martin, had grappled with a number of aches and pains in the years leading up to his imminent retirement.

As I walked alongside Brian, I became almost unaware of my surroundings, thinking instead about how much I had taken for granted, how little I had appreciated, or even truly savored. This was about more than just the little bit of fame I enjoyed; it was about the mere fact that until this week, I had been healthy and fit. It was about my having been naïve enough to operate as though it would last forever. I rewound through 2003 in my mind and thought about how many matches I had squandered or let go out of impatience or frustration. I thought about how little I had bothered to learn about all the cities I'd visited. I thought about how truly unique my position was, and yet it was not until then that I'd ever recognized it as such.

As we walked past the security checkpoint, the sight of my mother up ahead—unmistakable in her warm-up jacket and jeans, the large frames of her glasses popping against her sandy-blond hair—brought me back. Though athletic, my mom's a slight woman, with an ingrained British sense of modesty that can make her seem a bit withdrawn. In moments of concern, she appears downright frail, which is how she seemed to me when she spotted us and saw how I was shuffling along, and the way my head was squeezed up at the top of my neck by the brace.

I did what my father would have done and flashed a big, broad smile, letting her know that everything was all right.

We got to where she was standing and she gave me a gentle hug.

"Oh, James," she said, in her sweet, almost songlike voice. As she hugged Brian, she asked me: "Does it hurt?"

"I'm fine, Mom," I said. "Where's Dad?"

"Parking the car."

Having not had much of a conversation about the accident by phone, as we walked to baggage claim and waited with the other passengers, I gave my mother the blow-by-blow story of the last few days. She hung on every detail, shaking her head sadly from side to side, especially when I described the conflicting prognoses from the various doctors in Rome, which did little to change her less-than-complimentary opinion of the medical profession.

As I began to describe the flight home, my eye trained on a man coming in through the automatic doors, because I thought he looked like an older version of my father. It did not take long for me to realize that it *was* my father. Even from a distance, I could tell that the cancer was getting the best of him. A few months earlier, it had spread to his lungs, as stomach cancer often does. He had given up his stomach, but doctors can only remove the cancer they can see, and enough had remained to persist and to spread to other organs.

He got closer, and more details came into focus. In late January, I had been home, briefly, after the Australian Open, and the decline in his condition since then was instantly apparent and profound. The spring was gone from his step, his clothes hung off his frame in a way that he would only have allowed if the weight was dropping too quickly for his wardrobe to keep up. His face was thinning, the lines of his skull visible in the taut areas around his temples.

Clearly my Superman had met his kryptonite in this cancer, and he was no longer immune to the forces of our world, but it did little to bend his will. Just as I had done for my mom, he flashed me his trademark ear-to-ear smile—one-part happiness to see me, one-part reassurance, and with his looming hands outstretched he drew me into his comforting embrace.

"How are you feeling, James?" he asked, his voice as deep and joyous as ever.

As we waited for my bags to emerge from the mouth of the luggage carousel, my father—who craved details about any adverse situation so that he could set about solving it—began asking a million questions about my condition and the prognosis, but there was little that I could tell him. I didn't have many answers, and I wouldn't until I could see a doctor here in the States.

"Well," he said, patting me on the back, his hand feeling smaller, weaker than I remembered it, "we're happy you're home."

I was happy to be home, too. Being a traveling athlete will grow you up fast, but at the end of the day, I was still just twenty-four years old, and after what I had been through over the past few days, there was nobody I wanted to see more than my parents.

My mother and Brian joined in, and the focus of conversation moved from my neck injury onto more general catching up. Before long, our little foursome was cracking each other up. My father and I both put on quite a show, with me in my neck brace and him wasting away, and both of us laughing, carrying on like we didn't have a care in the world.

———————

We kept it up all the way back to Fairfield. Though the occasion was far from ideal, we had had no expectation of seeing each other until later in the summer, so this was an impromptu reunion, as much fun for Brian, who was like another member of the family, as it was for me and for them.

My parents dropped me off at my house. After the cryptic voice mail message that I'd left for them, Laura and Caraly were dying for details about what the hell had happened to me. I filled them in. I filled a lot of people in. In hindsight, I feel like I spent the entire weekend recounting the story to any number of friends, sitting in front of my computer checking e-mails, playing poker, and eagerly awaiting the arrival of my girlfriend, Katie. She had planned to visit me during the European clay-court season and was now planning a trip from California, where she had moved from her hometown of New Canaan.

On Monday, with the help of two doctors who work with the United States Davis Cup team, I made an appointment with Dr. Gregory Lutz, the head of physiatry at the Hospital for Special Surgery, near the East River on Manhattan's Upper East Side. Because my neck brace limited my ability to turn my head, making it unsafe for me to drive a car, and because they were as eager for details as I was, my parents drove me to the appointment.

Doctor Lutz performed a full examination: he removed my brace and gingerly felt around the neck area. He ordered a number of X-rays. He asked me all kinds of questions about the nature of the pain I felt and *where* I felt it. At the end of the visit, he told me that I had fractured a vertebra, number C-7 to be exact, explaining that the fracture was actually on one of the winglike pieces of the bone that flank the vertebral body. He also told me something that made my heart stop: if I hadn't turned my head just before impact, if I had smacked that net post straight on, the force very well might have left me paralyzed for life.

They say that tennis is a game of inches. So, I had just dis-covered, was life. If not for that reflexive move, my career would have been the least of my problems. As it was, Dr. Lutz told me that the fracture should heal within six to eight weeks. During that time, I was to wear the brace day and night, except in the shower, to refrain from exercise or exertion for the first several weeks, and to stop doing anything else that caused me pain or discomfort.

In the car on the way back from the city, I did some quick arithmetic in my head. Six weeks would put us into the third week of June. I speed-dialed Brian on my cell phone and told him the news: "That's just in time for Wimbledon," I said.

Brian didn't even have to have been in the doctor's office to know what was going on; it was my old positive-thinking taking control, my distinct talent for filtering out the bad news I wasn't interested in and focusing exclusively on the good: "James, that's best-case scenario. You can't even practice between now and then."

Though I didn't agree with his point of view, I was glad that my snapping at him back in Rome had done little to deter him from speaking his mind.

"We'll see," I told him.

Of course, as I describe this now, I realize that it sounds delusional, but my family's devotion to the upside of any sce-nario was such that I truly believed I could recuperate, hop across the Atlantic, and get right back on a tennis court against guys who would have been playing, more or less nonstop since the day I was first injured.

Another factor contributing to my optimism then was that as a teenager I had successfully overcome the debilitating and painful realities of scoliosis. When I was thirteen years old, during my annual medical checkup, the pediatrician detected what he thought was scoliosis. My parents took me to a chiropractor that they were just crazy about and whom they saw fairly regularly, hoping that he could fix the problem. To his credit, he told them that it was more than his discipline could correct, and he arranged for me to be seen at the Shriners Hospital for Children in Springfield, Massachusetts, about ninety minutes away by car, for an evaluation.

The Shriners Hospital for Children is part of a nonprofit network of pediatric hospitals throughout North America. When I think back on the one in Springfield, I almost forget that it was a not-for-profit operation because it was so state of the art and comfortable. When I went there for my evaluation, the doctors diagnosed me as having severe scoliosis, and their recommendation was to perform surgery, implanting a steel rod in my back to straighten it. It was a borderline call, but the procedure would have ended my tennis days, at least as a serious competitor, for good.

Now, at that point, we had absolutely no inkling that I'd

eventually become a professional tennis player. I was having a great time in the juniors (I had been the number one in the "twelve and unders" in New England the previous year), but because I was such a pipsqueak, now that I was in the next division, I was hovering around number four or five regionally and barely qualifying for national tournaments. But none of that mattered: I loved to play tennis, so we decided to take the alternative route and committed to my wearing a back brace—every day, all day— for four years.

My father's problem-solving instincts kicked in and he began researching scoliosis. Looking to do more than just the brace, everything he read said that sleeping on a firm surface would help correct the curvature, so he got rid of my bed, replacing it with a platform of cinderblocks topped by a piece of plywood and a thin cushion. It wasn't pretty, or comfortable, and it looked more like something that belonged in a prison cell than a kid's bedroom, but believe me when I tell you that I could feel my father's commitment and concern every time I lay down to sleep.

The doctors at the Shriners Hospital fitted me with a Boston brace, a full-body brace that ran roughly from my armpits to my tailbone. I wore it eighteen hours a day. I was never in any pain, but it was an uncomfortable existence because my back was kept as straight as a beam at all times. Sitting down was especially awkward. To keep the brace from itching, I wore a tight undershirt (the sleeveless tees that some people call "wifebeat-ers"), and to keep it from showing, I wore oversized shirts to school. The only time I didn't wear it was when I played tennis. I even wore it to bed, which was less than comfortable because we didn't have air-conditioning in the house in those days. By the time I woke up in the morning, the shirts I wore under it would be damp with sweat, and they stained in record time, forcing us to replenish my supply constantly.

If you've ever seen me on a tennis court, screaming up to my box after a big point, or at the end of a match, then you wouldn't believe how shy I was as a kid, and the back brace only made me more so. I had my friends, but I was still a small fry, about five feet three inches at age fifteen, and the brace made me feel like a bit of a freak, like I had a secret to protect, and I did a pretty good job of concealing it. Only my friends knew about it—my friends and anyone who happened to brush up against me in the hallway at school.

Throughout all of this the Shiners Hospital was amazing. During the four years I wore the brace, I was constantly growing into new sizes, and each time I did—including during my super spurt at age fifteen, when I zoomed through three of them in about a year—they replaced it happily and free of charge, ac-cording to their charitable mission. This was no small thing to our family, as the braces were worth about a thousand dollars apiece—I'm sure my parents would have found a way to buy them if they had to, but it would have been a strain, to be sure.

In addition to the medical and financial support it provided me, the Shriners Hospital kept me from feeling sorry for myself. The doctors there saw all kinds of patients, from very young children with cleft lips and palates to those with third-degree burns. Every time I went for a visit, I witnessed children my own age, and much, much younger, being wheeled in and out of surgery, being fitted for prosthetic limbs, or undergoing physical therapy. It was a powerful experience for a little kid to have. I know that the injured and the handicapped are often scary to children, and can even make adults uncomfortable, but I was fascinated by these children, kids my own age, being wheeled around or straining to lift a weight. Seeing them and their strength made me grateful that my problems were so minor compared to theirs, and I was moved by their determination. They seemed to me to be living proof of my father's feelings about hard work and never letting circumstances get you down.

When I was seventeen, I stopped going to the hospital, and though they treated it to the fullest extent possible, my scoliosis was not completely cured. I still have lingering effects from it— my walk is a little funny, and if I sit for a long time or in backless chairs or run on uneven surfaces, I get some aching in my upper back. I've also slept on the floor in some four- and five-star hotels. If the mattress is too soft, I'm just more comfortable there, so I gather up my pillows and my comforter and crash on the carpet.

There's a chance that I'll eventually have the surgery I skipped as a kid because the scoliosis will get worse as I get older. They say that tennis is a sport for life, so I'll have to play that one by ear.

The result of this entire back trauma was that I always considered myself pretty darn lucky to be on a tennis court at all, having worn a back brace for four years to make that possible. As such, six *weeks* with a neck brace wasn't particularly daunting to me because I had spent time in a brace before—much more time in a much bigger brace. I was bummed that I wouldn't be able to play in the French Open, and that I wouldn't make the Olympic team that year, but the bottom line was that having a broken, or nearly broken, neck, while it sounds very dramatic, in my case actually wasn't much worse than having a bad ankle sprain.

Because the neck brace Dr. Lutz gave me was so large and firm, made of hard, sloping plastic with a rubber collar to provide at least a little comfort, I couldn't turn my neck left and right, so I still couldn't drive myself to the hospital. Brian, always happy to help out, and eager to get the facts firsthand, took me to my second visit at the Hospital for Special Surgery, about a week later. As usual, he heard everything, the bad along with the good, which verified his hunch that my Wimbledon dreams for that year were just that—dreams.

When we left the doctor's office, he turned to me and echoed what he'd told me on the phone a week earlier, "James, the doctor said you *might* be okay, but you can't even practice before then."

What could I say? He was right. My next tournament appearance would have to wait until the summer hard-court season and the buildup to the US Open in August.

———

As far as my career was concerned, the next several weeks were a washout. I couldn't run or lift weights, and the truth of the matter is that I became pretty slothful: My roommates would see me eating cereal in the living room in the morning, then I'd spend the day playing online poker and watching *SportsCenter* on ESPN. When they came home after work, they'd find me right where they left me. They began to joke that I never moved, and the truth wasn't that far off.

But although I didn't discuss it very much, there was something I did several days each week that did take me outside the house: I went across town to visit my father. On many days, around lunchtime, my mother or my brother (and sometimes my girlfriend, Katie, for the short time she was visiting) would pick me up and drive me the ten minutes or so to my parents' house. As I healed enough to drive myself, I began going every day, stopping by D'Angelo's, a local restaurant, on the way over to pick up some lunch.

During these drives, I had the most profound sense of the past meeting the present. I would pass places that I had known my whole life, like the storefront on Kings Highway that used to be Applause Video. That storefront was my first memory of Fairfield, having slept on the drive up from Yonkers when we moved to Connecticut and awakened just as our car was passing the video store. Applause closed years ago, and though the space was now occupied by a patio furniture store, I still felt as though I could make out the Applause logo on the facade.

Memories like this from my entire time in Fairfield would draw me into a current of emotion. But as I got closer to my parents' home, the house where I grew up and where my bedroom still had posters of Michael Jordan on the wall, the reality of where I was and what was going on would settle in and I'd sink back down. Sitting in the car at the intersection of my past, present, and future forced me into recollections I hadn't had in years and caused me to enjoy each and every moment as they passed. The more I did that drive, the more it stretched and changed, the more it became something else altogether. These were more than simply the moments before I arrived at my parents' house; these were the moments when I was developing a new respect and appreciation for the concept of time.

Time is a remarkably strange thing in that it's the one thing that you can't get back. You can rehab an injury, lose weight, resolve conflicts, pay off debts, and fix just about anything else in your world. But once time slips away, it's gone forever. And yet, there I was, spending more time at home than I had since I was nineteen, just enjoying the opportunity to be with my father. Driving over to their house constantly, it wasn't long before I realized that I had been handed a golden opportunity, the chance to do what's usually impossible: to regain time.

I've had a lot of good fortune in my life, but when I look back on the summer of 2004, I realize that the luckiest thing that ever happened to me was fracturing my neck on that steel net post in Rome. I was only twenty-four, but I had already been swept up into my professional world for five years. The life of a professional athlete bears little resemblance to that of a business executive, but in some ways, they're remarkably similar: I was consumed with my work, I was on the road all the time, and when I wasn't playing, I was down in Tampa working out and practicing.

My injury gave me the gift of time that otherwise I never would have had, and I decided to seize it. In many ways, we seemed to be living in our own little world that spring—I was around during the core of the tennis season and my father, who had never missed a day of work in his life, was home all the time. And we'd visit during business hours, when the neighborhood was a ghost town, silent but for the occasional laughter of kids coming home from school or a dog barking in a nearby yard. It was not an eerie silence but a calming one; during the spring and summer my parents kept their front door open, and on these quiet afternoons you could hear the wind blowing gently through the living room.

I'd park outside and walk into the house. My mother would meet me downstairs and tell me how things had been going that morning, then she'd take off to run her daily errands and I'd climb up to the second floor. More often than not, I visited my father in their bedroom, which was the small room at the end of the hall. It was a safe place, a place where you could hear my parents laughing at night or the sound of my father doing his push-ups in the morning, but by then it had become decidedly sad. The details hadn't changed, the bed was still centered against a wall next to the window, and the television was positioned right next to the door. Their tiny closet was overflowing with clothes, and there was an old chair in the corner that had probably been there since my parents bought the place. And, as always, my father had a book or two on his nightstand.

But the cancer had taken over the room, as surely as it had taken over Dad's body. There was an IV bag, held aloft on a pole, by which he was "fed" the high-protein liquid that now made up his diet, and crates of the liquid in little plastic pouches were piled up off to the side. There were also vitamins on his nightstand, which he had begun to take in his willingness to try any-thing to get better.

We settled into a rhythm over those weeks. Sometimes we'd just sit together. Sometimes we'd reminisce. We talked about the first time he came to Wimbledon, which oddly enough was also my first time there, about how my mother had delighted in showing us off to her relatives and showing her country off to us. I don't know if my father would have enjoyed visiting En-gland on his own; he was always happiest when other people were happy. With me playing in Wimbledon and my mother's unabashed excitement to be home, there was a lot of happiness going around, and so that trip was just heaven for him.

One thing we did *not* talk about was his condition, but there were moments during every visit when his frailty was un-deniable. When he got up out of his chair to go to the bathroom, the mere act of rising required tremendous effort. One time, he changed his shirt in front of me, and his body was so emaci-ated—the skin hugging each rib on both sides of his chest—that I turned away, not in disgust, but to help him maintain his dig-nity. Sometimes a nurse would come in and implement various tests and exercises to monitor and improve, where possible, his day-to-day health. In one exercise, she had him blow into a spi-rometer, a form of pulmonary therapy intended to expand the lungs to their full capacity, which helps prevent bacteria from collecting there and causing pneumonia, a big concern with lung cancer. This was the same man whose early-morning exercises filled our home every morning when I was growing up, who would follow a full day at the office with a round of golf or a few sets of tennis. Now he had to work just to expand his lungs.

As I sat there and watched him struggle to inhale large breaths of air, I found myself returning to the thoughts I had as I was shuffling through the airport right after Brian and I touched down at JFK. While then I had been focused on the short shelf life of my own youth, now I was becoming consumed with thoughts of how potentially fleeting *everything* was. For the first time in my life that I could remember, I was beginning to develop a respect for fate. It was a grudging respect at best, but I couldn't escape the irony of my father's situation: a nonsmoking, nondrinking vegetarian, who was remarkably fit—even as he entered his late fifties—and possessed of a peerless sense of determination, was nonetheless clearly losing his fight with this disease.

I thought back to how vital and imposing a figure my father had been just over a year earlier. I imagined him engaged in his daily routine back then, driving along the highways and byways of Connecticut, smiling behind the wheel of his car, enjoying the simple beauty of that time. I imagined him shaking hands with his 3M contact at a hospital and catching up with him on his personal life before delving into business. I thought about him playing tennis and golf and loving every second of it.

And I thought about how much he must have missed those things and yet how happy he still managed to seem.

When the nurse left, he saw the distressed look on my face, and laughed.

"I guess you haven't seen me like that yet," he said. "Don't worry, James, we'll figure something out."

Even when I was a little boy, my father would tell me to never burden those close to me with my own problems. "If you have a problem, you *fix* it," he'd tell me. But I never realized how absolutely devoted to this ideal he was. He was physically weaker than I'd ever imagined was possible, but he'd never seemed more superhuman to me.

———

And that was how the days passed during May and June.

But nights, well, nights were a different story.

During that summer, my social life in Fairfield wasn't all that different from life on a college campus, only we lived in houses rather than dorms, and most of my friends spent their days at work rather than in class. We were also several years older than your average undergrad, but we tried not to think about that.

When the sun went down, we all hung out wherever the action happened to be that night, usually my place, or Evan's house right around the corner, which he shared with his housemate, Matt Daly, a former top junior player from Massachusetts who was my doubles partner way back when.

Over the years there were a lot of people who came and went in our group, but there was always a core of regulars, many of whom are still friends now. There was J. P. Johnson, Evan's best friend from college, who I got to be friendly with at the French Open a few years back and was teaching at a country club near his home in Rye, New York. My brother was in and out of town, crashing either on my couch or back in his old bedroom at my parents' house. Andy Jorgensen, Brian's best friend since childhood, lived about five minutes away in Fairfield and often dropped by. We also had visits from Al and Mike Nelson, who lived down by the beach, my golfing buddy Kevin Henry, who played golf at the University of Tulsa, and Paco Fabian, another guy I played tennis with in the juniors and who also roomed with Evan and Matt.

Some combination of this group would be around on any given night for spontaneous visits and late-night rap sessions fueled by beer and pizza. The other ingredient in these evenings was poker, which was beginning to become a major obsession of mine. If there were just a few of the guys hanging out, we might each be playing an online game on our individual laptops, or we might get around the table for some "live" poker. If the group was more coed, then we'd skip the poker and just hang.

For very different reasons, I treasured these evenings almost as much as I did the time with my father. Just as I was making the most of this unexpected but crucial time with my father, my injury was giving me the opportunity to relax with my friends and enjoy a collegial scene that I had abandoned midway through college. I really only got to see my friends when I was home for the US Open (and then just barely) and during Christmas, so once again I found myself making up for lost time.

The cruel joke of it all was that I knew it couldn't last. While people often delude themselves into thinking that something like this can go on forever, I did not have that luxury. My life had come to consist of borrowed time, and sooner or later reality would be unavoidable.

As those weeks wore on, there was a bittersweet dichotomy at work: my physical condition was improving, while my father's was deteriorating. More and more, he had to breathe through an oxygen generator (a huge apparatus, parked near my parents' bed, that raises the oxygen level in the air it sends through a tube) and would take along a backpack tank when he and my mother left the house. On one harrowing evening, we were driving home from a fortieth birthday party for one of the pros from the tennis club, and the tank nearly ran out, forcing us to screech up to the curb and scramble into the house to hook Dad up to the generator.

Meanwhile, my neck had healed to the point that Dr. Lutz was comfortable fitting me for a smaller brace, which allowed me to swivel my head, enabling me to drive but further exposing the imbalance between my father's condition and mine. Now, instead of him driving me to the doctor, it was my turn to drive him to his appointments at Memorial Sloan-Kettering Cancer Center. Even in his increasingly weary state, with the oxygen tank perpetually at his side, he maintained the role of the patriarch; when we'd pull into a garage, or I'd stop off for a slice of pizza, he'd insist on paying.

He kept his spirits up remarkably well, but his body was starting to give out. In addition to the periodic checkups, he began staying overnight at the hospital once in a while, then staying for two nights. He must have been worried, but he kept it all to himself. "They just want to keep me here," he'd say, sounding almost bemused at the idea that he couldn't come home. "I'm not really sure why." When he returned from these stays, he'd go right back to his positive ways, at least as much as he could. But he was clearly getting weaker all the time.

Still, he did whatever he could to keep up appearances. One of his most Herculean efforts was his participation in the most everyday occasion, when Katie and her mom, who lived in nearby New Canaan, came to dinner at my parents' house. Dad could have easily chosen to stay upstairs in his bedroom, and nobody would have blamed him or felt the least bit slighted. Instead, he came to the table, oxygen tank and all, and was the life of the party, asking questions of our guests and showering them with attention. During that meal, the spirit of Thomas Blake Sr. was alive and well, and clearly he was going to keep it that way for as long as his body could fight the fight. When Katie and her mom said good night, and we shut the door behind them, the toll the performance took on my father was unmistakable: he was so fatigued that I thought his knees might buckle.

Through this and other similar displays, he kept uttering what had almost become his motto that spring: "I'm going to beat this." While his increasingly emaciated frame told a different story, there was a huge part of me that wanted desperately to believe, and as such I let myself believe him. I believed him because of the conviction with which he said it. I believed him because of the effort he poured into maintaining as normal a life as possible. And, let's be honest, I believed him because he was my father, my Superman, and he'd always done whatever he said he would.

———

In mid-June, I went to see Dr. Lutz in New York for another in a series of periodic checkups. After weeks of hoping for the green light, he finally said the words I'd been waiting to hear: "I think it'd be okay for you to jog a little."

As soon as I got back to Fairfield, I hit the local gym and

got right on the treadmill. Though I was still supposed to wear the brace most of the time, Dr. Lutz okayed my removing it during exercise. I began by walking, slowly working up to a light jog, and then a medium-paced run. It felt great to be running. The sweat began to come, and I could feel the sensation of my shirt soaking it up like a sponge, becoming wet and heavy against my skin. I had to towel off for the first time in weeks. Before I knew it, I had run three miles.

But when I stopped and cooled down, I was tighter than usual, and by the time I pulled into my driveway, my back and neck were beginning to ache. I called Dr. Lutz.

"I said you could jog *a little,*" he said, clearly alarmed and admonishing me for my overzealousness.

I pulled back a little on my next visit to the gym, but my appetite for competition was ravenous. Within days, I was hitting with Brian, my first time on the court in over a month. It was amazing just to be out there, but it had been so long since I had played, that I got blisters on my fingers. But our hit went well enough that I set my sights on playing the annual grass court tournament at the International Tennis Hall of Fame in Newport, Rhode Island, the week after Wimbledon ended. Instantaneously, that tournament in Rhode Island became the new focus for my game. In my mind, I began to hear that long-lost sound, the voice of an announcer crackling through the public address system: *"Ladies and gentlemen, from Fairfield, Connecticut, please welcome James Blake!"*

Unfortunately, this rush of enthusiasm and good news was countered by bad news for my father. No sooner had I been given the green light to start working out again than my father, mother, and I sat in a doctor's office at Sloan-Kettering and heard the ominous declaration, "We'll need to go back to the original drugs."

The news hit us like a slap in the face; it was the doctors' way of telling us that those experimental drugs weren't having the desired effect.

My mother spoke for all of us: "What's next?"

The moment of silence that followed said more than the eventual sentence: "We'll go back to the original drugs and hope for the best."

Hope for the best. It had about as much real meaning as something uttered by a political spokesperson. It was a nothing statement, the empty promise of someone who was just looking to fill the air with a positive word like *hope*. The unspoken meaning was clear: the doctors were giving up on my dad. We looked at one another as our hearts caught in our throats.

"Well then that's what we'll do," said my father, and we thanked the doctors and left. But I knew we were all having the same thought: things were moving backward. It was so unlike us for that to happen. Our family placed such a premium on work and its ability to create progress. Work could get you through anything, couldn't it? Hard work and determination. Wasn't that enough to make anything true? Wasn't that enough to keep my father alive for as long as he was willing to keep at it?

If only the doctors had given us instructions. If only they had said, "Do this, and this and this and this, Mr. Blake," he would have done it. But they didn't because, simply put, he was all out of options. Once again it was fate having its way with us. Something was happening and it was not of our doing. I was becoming aware, for the first time really, that sometimes bad things happen to good people for no discernable reason.

In the car on the way home, we tried to keep the conversation light. Despite the day's devastating development, we chose to stay positive, at least outwardly. Even in the face of all this, Dad still kept up his hopeful demeanor and never showed any fear or signs of wavering confidence. For that very reason, I headed down to my house in Tampa a few days later to send him a sign that even with the news, I wasn't afraid to leave him there, that I wasn't fearful that I wouldn't see him again. I was, of course, but my brother would be in Fairfield for a while, so he could help out, keep my mom company, and send up the Bat-Signal if I needed to hurry back.

When I first arrived in Tampa, I was glad to get back and catch up with my buds there, but I quickly learned that it's much harder to be away from somebody when they're sick than it is to be with them. My new feeling of powerlessness was magnified exponentially. I'd have done anything to help my father, but I wasn't a part of his medical equation, and from that distance, all I could do was wonder when the next bit of bad news would come rolling in.

It didn't take long: I was on the computer in my home office three nights later when Thomas called me on my cell phone.

"Dad's in the hospital again," he said. "He's in for good now. He's not going to come back." I later learned that the doctors were no longer able to manage the amount of carbon dioxide that periodically built up in his lungs due to the cancer there. They expected the situation to get steadily and swiftly worse, and so the consensus was that under these circumstances, the hospital would be the best option for him.

We hung up and I just sat there staring at the screen. I don't know for how long. My first impulse was to head right for the airport and get on the next flight that would put me anywhere near Fairfield, but I knew that my father wouldn't want me to do that. I had a full summer of tennis coming up, and he'd prefer that I get back in shape so that I could perform at my best when the time came. It was a tough reality to swallow, but there wasn't a doubt in my mind that he wanted it this way.

I woke up the next morning to one of those perfect Florida

mornings: hot but not excessively humid, with a light breeze and not a cloud in the sky. Brian and I had a running joke that pokes fun at our own over-the-top optimism: when we meet at the courts, if it's even a halfway-decent day, I'll ask him, "Nicest day of the year, Brian?" and he'll say back, "Nicest day of the year."

This actually *was* one of the nicest mornings of the year, but when I thought of my father, lying helpless in his spartan hospital room up North and how he'd never again be able to experience the outdoors, my spirit sank low, lower than it had ever been in my life.

Nonetheless, I did what Dad would want me to do: I went over to the practice courts and began hitting with Mardy and Jeff, but I couldn't muster more than a lackluster effort. I was going through the motions, the mere mechanics, of hitting the ball, of running around the backcourt, of moving in for a volley, but it was a sullen, joyless performance. My mind was elsewhere—specifically, it was in my father's room up in Bridgeport, Connecticut. I felt a tremendous sense of being pulled back there, of almost physically having to resist the urge to bolt off the court and head home. I was trying, as hard as I knew how, to honor my father's wishes, but it was painful not to be there with him and the rest of my family.

Kevin O'Connor, Saddlebrook's executive director, walked by and saw me halfheartedly slapping at the ball, without my usual focus and grunting effort. Kevin's an intense guy who can be tenacious about his work, but he also has a warm side, and seeing me out there brought it to the surface.

"James," he said, sounding almost amused. "What are you doing?"

I stopped hitting and walked over to the edge of the court. I guess I had been keeping a lot inside, because I really opened up and told him about my father, and how he was in the hospital . . . for good.

After laying it all out for Kevin and hearing my thoughts spoken aloud, I realized that I had no place being on that court, and so I did something else I never do: I stopped practice early and went home. Back at my house I didn't know what to do with myself. It was an odd feeling. I was usually so focused, but not that day. I couldn't decide what to do. What I wanted, of course, was to make my father better. But no amount of work was going to make that happen. The idea of working out or playing tennis seemed like a joke. The only thing to do, it seemed, was to get back to Fairfield.

The next day or two went by in an instant as I made my preparations to return to Connecticut. It was like a cut in a movie: one second I was in my house in Tampa, the next I was in an elevator on my way up to my father's room in Bridgeport Hospital, where he had gone to die.

Hospitals have a way of imposing reality on you, with their institutional hallways, the sameness of the rooms, and by this point, the condition of the patient. I couldn't believe how much my father had deteriorated in just a few days. Not only was he even smaller than he was when I left town, but because he couldn't get enough oxygen into his lungs, and because carbon dioxide would build up there, he would slip in and out of consciousness.

Seeing him like that caused a seismic shift in my world: as much as I wanted to return to the tour, and as much as *he* wanted me to start playing again, I suddenly just didn't care about it anymore, at least not for now. Standing there beside his bed, watching him come and go involuntarily, I simply didn't care about hearing that announcer's voice I'd been fantasizing about. All I wanted to do was to spend as much time as possible with my father.

"Dad, Thomas and I are going to pull out of Newport," I told him during one of his more cognizant moments.

"Absolutely not," he told me, putting as much force behind his voice as he could muster, seeming almost as if he were going to stand up out of bed in protest. "You two get on with your life. I'll be fine."

I still didn't want to go, but I wasn't going to argue with him. My father had spoken and, as always, I would do as he said. End of discussion.

In his final days, my father reminded me of a boxer who kept getting back on his feet, no matter how many times he'd been knocked down. Friends would call and he'd spend ten minutes on the phone with them, telling them he felt fine and asking them what was going on in their lives, then as soon as he'd hang up, he'd be totally spent and would nod off.

Curiously, when he was fully awake, he was as relaxed as I'd ever seen him. My mother, my brother, and I would take turns being with him, and the conversation was surprisingly light and relaxed. Occasionally, he'd make a point of reiterating, for what he knew might be the final time, that he was proud of me, and of Thomas, but otherwise, except for the setting, it almost seemed like old times as I caught him up on how my practices were going, and what was going on with my roommates and other friends. Or we'd sit and watch a Mets game on television, and in the dim blue light it cast on the hospital room, I felt like we were back enjoying a summer night in our family home.

But the decline continued, and before long he was not only nodding off more frequently, he was becoming disoriented, talking to people that weren't there or saying things that didn't make sense. Maybe he was reliving past moments or was halfway asleep and dreaming. I have no idea, but it was difficult to watch.

It was clear that he was putting the pieces together much as we were. He set aside some time with the father of one of Thomas's closest friends to go over his will, the first outward sign that he was coming to terms with the inevitable.

And still, in his lucid moments, my father refused to be a drain on us. "Go home, James. Get some rest," he'd tell me. Usually I'd stay anyway, but sometimes, I'd think he was right, and that I really did need the rest.

One night, after a reluctant departure, I drove back to my house. I walked inside. Laura was there. I stood in the doorway and told her about what was going on, about how my father was, for all intents and purposes, gone.

I didn't know it at the time, but I was already in a state of mourning. I was fixated and stunted, unable to do anything but think of my father and let the reality of the situation sink in. Each day it seemed to hit me harder, as though the trials of the previous day were not enough and my pain could not get any worse. I was exhausted and I was drained of everything but my sadness. I went upstairs, collapsed on the bed, and started sobbing. Laura came up and sat down next to me.

"We're all here for you, James," she said. "You have so many friends. You have so much to look forward to." And then she said the best thing anyone could have said: "Your dad did such a good job raising you."

Even my friends knew that the most comforting thing one

could say about my dad was how much of an impact he had made on someone else's life. It surely would have made him smile to hear that.

————

On the morning of Friday, July 2, I called my father and he said something that he never had in all his days of being sick: "James, I want you to get over here."

I was out the door in a shot, screeched out of the driveway, and next thing I knew I was standing breathless in the doorway of his hospital room.

"Hi, Dad," I said.

He was very focused and determined: "James," he said. "I know this is it. I know my time here is gone."

This was the first time he had said these words to me, and I felt the air go out of my lungs. But he looked me right in the eye, giving me the strength to do what he needed me to: "Call your mother. I need you to call your mother. It's getting tougher."

I picked up the bedside phone and called Mom at work.

My mother answered.

"Mom, it's James."

She could hear in my voice that something was wrong: "What is it?"

"Mom, you need to get over here. Now. I don't care if they have to close the club."

She said she was on her way and I hung up. I pulled a chair over to my father's bedside and we sat there together. We didn't talk. There was nothing left to say. I had the feeling he was already halfway out of this world.

I couldn't help it, a few tears streamed down my face.

"It's going to be okay," he said, and I nodded.

"I know."

Light poured in through the windows and the bed cast a long shadow on the floor. In the bright stillness of the room, we sat huddled together, our words uneasily hushed and my head draped near his body.

When my mother arrived, suddenly there was no holding back for any of us. All of the days when we let optimism do our talking, all of the hours we passed putting on our best faces suddenly came tumbling down in front of us. Our hope had gotten us far, a lot farther than it might have for most people, but it had not carried the day, and for the first time as a group we acknowledged the reality that lay before us. All at once, we let loose a torrent of emotion—we were unabashedly crying, and my parents were holding hands and looking into each other's eyes—an incredible display from two people who had never been especially expressive.

In the midst of all of this, my father told me, for what he

knew was the last time, how proud he was of me, and I told him I loved him and that he had made me a man and that whatever I had done and would do would all be because of him.

He smiled, fighting to keep his composure, and nodded. Sitting there, the only sound in the room was that of the three of us breathing, one breath in and another one out. Inhaling and exhaling, the routine of life.

And then, because he had insisted, because it was my routine, and because it was my life that he continued to shape, I pulled myself together, said good-bye for the last time, hugged my mom hard, and left to go to Newport, Rhode Island, to play tennis.

————

Brian drove to Newport. I sat in the passenger seat and neither of us said a thing. When words might be useful, Brian has the right ones. But he also knows that there are times when the best thing you can say to somebody is nothing at all. I was strung out and exhausted, staring into the summer night and thinking that it felt more like winter—cold and lonely. Then I fell asleep.

A few hours later, Brian and I were waiting in line to check into our hotel in Newport. The lobby was filling up with players, coaches, and a few journalists, and standing there among them after so many months of separation felt surreal. Being half asleep from my nap only made it more dreamlike, to be back on the scene under such painful circumstances.

Somebody shouted: "Can you believe this?"

Brian and I turned around and saw that one of the guys from the tour, a player I'm actually pretty friendly with, was getting into it pretty good with the desk clerk.

We made eye contact: "James, can you believe this?" he said to me, throwing his arms up in disgust and making a real scene. "My plane was late and now my room isn't ready."

I just stared at him.

"Amazing!" he yelled, glaring at the clerk.

My eyes narrowed. I was angry. I wanted to tell him to shut up, that my father was about to expire on a hospital bed back home, that I actually had my hand on my cell phone in my pocket so that I would feel it if it began to vibrate with the news. I wanted to scream that I was grateful that my neck was in one piece and that I was about to get out on the court for the first time since May.

He kept laying into the guy.

I wanted to tell him to take a look around at how lucky he was to do what he did for a living. If he wasn't blessed with talent, he might have to work a more conventional job, maybe at a hotel like this, where he might get chewed out by some athlete who found waiting for his bed to be made to be a hardship.

I was seriously thinking about laying into *him*, when I

caught Brian staring right into my eyes and shaking his head almost imperceptibly from left to right so that only I would notice it. He knew *exactly* what I was thinking and was telling me not to do it.

I decided to keep my mouth shut.

"May I help the next guest, please," said a woman at another station along the front desk, and Brian and I moved up to the front of the line.

"James, your father died this morning."

The news was delivered by a voice mail, left on my cell phone by my mother, her voice quivering as she reminded me of his wishes for Thomas and me to stay in the tournament.

It was Saturday, July 3. I normally don't leave my phone on at night, but I was expecting to hear from her at any moment from the time I left the hospital. In the middle of the night, my phone buzzed to announce a text message, and I shot up in bed. It was a note from a long-lost friend, clearly drunk and not at all aware of what was going on in my life. I had forgotten my charger, and I was afraid my phone's battery would die before morning, so I turned it off. When I woke up and turned it on, that's when I got my mother's message.

As I was listening to it, my brother showed up in the doorway of my room.

"Did you get the message from Mom?" he asked.

I just nodded. As usual, we didn't need to say anything: we just put our heads down and headed to the hotel restaurant for breakfast. We met Brian there and told him what had happened. He said he was sorry and we all opened our newspapers and silently ate. I peered up at one point to look around at all the faces in the room, some of them familiar, and thought how none of them knew what a monumental event had just occurred in our lives.

That very afternoon, my brother did what my father had asked him to: he went out and won his qualifying match seven to six in the third set over Croat Dusan Vemic. I'd never been prouder of Thomas and the way he stepped up that day, making all the right decisions and going for his shots right into the third-set tie break.

On Monday, it was my turn, and it was about as un-ideal a scenario as I could ask for: the grass courts in Newport keep the ball low, with some spots here and there that produce bad bounces, and my opponent was someone who would almost certainly not allow me to get into a rhythm—a red-headed Belgian named Dick Norman who's well over six feet tall and has a booming serve.

I was in mourning, and lacked the confidence that comes with playing regularly, but I really wanted to win for my mother, who had made the drive up from home and was in the stands, along with her sister, Phyllis, whom we all call "Nin," who had flown in from Missouri to be with her.

I also wanted to win for my dad, who I firmly believe was looking over me.

I took the match one precarious step at a time. I knew that if I could get my returns in play, I'd have a chance.

Though I had been looking forward to getting back out on a court, it was a bittersweet afternoon, to say the least. When the announcer said those magic words, "from Fairfield, Connecticut, let's have a nice hand for James Blake," I didn't enjoy them at all. I just couldn't fully engage in the fun of competition. Late in the first set, Norman came in after a drop shot I hit, and his momentum, coupled with the fact that he's as tall as a guy on stilts, made it impossible for him to stop at the net. Instead he leaped over it, and, finding himself on my side, barreled at me like he was going to knock me down. The crowd loved it, and while I knew it was funny, I couldn't even enjoy that moment.

Plain and simple, I was on a mission that afternoon: my father wanted me to win this match, and I was going to win it for him.

I won the first set in a squeaker, edging Norman out 9–7 in a tie break, but rather than get excited, I stayed calm and methodical, maintaining my composure all the way through the second set, which I won more comfortably, 6–3, largely thanks to my bread-and-butter shot, my forehand, which was starting to click again.

Despite how much I wanted this win, I didn't really celebrate the victory. It was a relief, maybe the biggest relief I'd ever known on a tennis court, but it didn't bring me any relief from the sadness that consumed me. When it was all over, I shook Norman's hand and located my mother in the crowd—she could tell from my expression that this win was for her, and she smiled sadly and nodded.

On the heels of our victories, Thomas and I decided to do something else to honor our father's memory; or rather, we decided *not* to do something else. Neither of us mentioned to the media that my father had died. There was no way Dad would have wanted this to turn into a pity party for his two sons.

Before my mother left to go back home, she handed Thomas and me a 3M envelope. Tucked inside was a handwritten note from my father to me and Thomas, scribbled in his last days, telling us one last time how proud he was of us, just to be sure that we got the message.

I lost my next match to Alex Bogomolov Jr., but I didn't mind being out of the tournament. I knew that I was way too rusty to win the whole thing, and by that point, I wanted to get back home and help plan my father's funeral service. When I got off the court after the loss, though, my arm was killing me, and I ended up doing the post-match press conference with a bag of ice on it. I went to see a doctor and discovered that I had a strained bicep, a common spring-training injury in baseball pitchers, brought on by pushing the muscle hard after a long period of inactivity. It was a logical injury, if there is such a thing, but I also felt vaguely under the weather, and I began to think that I might be coming down with something.

But there was no time to dwell on any of that. With my father's funeral just two days away, there was a lot of work to be done.

———

You really learn who your friends are by how well they show up at a down time. I received a ton of cards, some of which actually gave me solace—like the one from an IMG agent who wrote me a note about how pain eventually fades, but good memories last forever. My mother's best friend, Erica Ceccarelli, made me some snacks and cooked me dinner one night during these days, as did my friend Andy's wife, Kristie Jorgensen. I was also moved to receive phone calls from a number of the other players on the tour and some old friends from college who had heard the news.

My father's funeral was held at St. Anthony's Church, an intimate, relatively modern-looking house of worship on Pine

Creek Road in Fairfield that Friday, and when I got there I couldn't believe my eyes: there were about a hundred people, including "business" friends who had traveled great distances to attend. My agent, Carlos, had cut his vacation short to fly in from Greece; Todd Martin and his coach, Rick Ferman, had made the trip; Mike Nakajima from Nike in Oregon; and Davis Cup captain Patrick McEnroe were there as well. I was also shocked to see that all my friends who lived in the area were there. I had made a point of not telling them about the funeral because I didn't want them cashing in vacation or personal days to attend, but somehow they all found out and were standing there in the rows behind me.

Thomas spoke, delivering a eulogy about my father's lessons and how they had made him a man, then I took to the dais and talked about my father in the only way I knew how—as the hero that he was. I spoke of how as a little kid I thought of him as Superman, and how I secretly never stopped thinking of him that way, even after I had gone off to Harvard, then become a professional athlete. Even after the magazine and television pieces and the modeling. Even as a full-grown adult, I had never stopped thinking of my father as Superman.

The problem was, I said, that Superman isn't supposed to die, so my goal would be to find a way to make him immortal. There were all kinds of ways to do this, I said: I could get a tattoo or build a statute, but those things crumble or fade away.

Fighting back tears, I explained that my way of making sure my father was immortal would be to live my life by his example, and when I had kids I would make sure that they lived by his example as well. The same would be true for their kids as well, and so on down the line.

In that way, I figured, my father really would live forever.

FOUR

FIVE MINUTES OF HITTING, TWENTY-FIVE MINUTES OF TALKING

JULY–SEPTEMBER 2004

Perseverance is not a long race; it is many short races one after the other.

—WALTER ELLIOT

It was, of course, a blue weekend following my father's funeral, and I spent almost every waking moment thinking about him and how much I'd miss him. I knew that he wouldn't have wanted me to dwell on his absence, that more than anything he'd want me to get on with my life and get back to work, but I needed those days, just a few of them, to begin to figure out how to function in a world without him in it.

I also needed some time for my bicep to recover. Because of the injury, I had to pull out of a tournament in Los Angeles the following week, which was a bit of a letdown, since it was one of the first of the US hard-court events. Hard courts are the tennis surface that I play best on, and I'd been dreaming of American concrete since I first learned how long my neck would take to heal.

On Monday, I got back to work, meeting Brian at the courts at Fairfield University. We didn't talk much, and because of the bicep, I couldn't serve. We went through a series of drills, and then I left.

Tuesday was just as efficient and just as joyless.

On Wednesday morning, I woke up in bed on the second floor of my house in Fairfield and knew right away that something was wrong. My head was throbbing with an internal pounding so severe that it took me a while before I realized that it was confined to the left side, from my ear up and back into the cranium. I hadn't exactly bounded out of bed for the past several days, but that morning I felt bone tired, and as I eased into consciousness, I realized that I also had a sore throat. Swallowing repeatedly to probe it, I determined that it, too, was confined to the left side.

This all seemed pretty strange, but I was supposed to be back in workout mode, so I threw on a T-shirt and shorts, laced up my sneaks, and got into my car. I couldn't shake the feeling that the left-side-only pain was cause for concern, so I swung by the walk-in clinic in town and described my symptoms to the doctor, who figured I had contracted some kind of bacterial infection and prescribed an antibiotic. I wasn't one for medicine, but I went along with his recommendation and swallowed the first one on the way to Fairfield University, where Brian was waiting for me.

We hit for about fifteen minutes. I thought that maybe once I got some fresh air in my lungs and my blood was pumping, I'd be able to work through whatever was ailing me and be able to practice. But it wasn't only the pain; I just felt *off*. It was hard to place what it was, but I wasn't moving right. There wasn't much juice on my ground strokes. And I felt shaky and weak. A little voice told me it was time to stop.

"I'm not feeling well, Brian."

I told him about the symptoms I'd woken up with, and about the clinic.

"I need to stop."

He was incredulous. It was simply unheard of for me to stop practicing. He's never been an especially good actor, and that day there was absolutely no hiding his concern.

We called it quits and I drove home.

When I saw Evan later that day, I told him about my

symptoms. He looked a little sheepish about it, then revealed that because he had recently recovered from tonsillitis, he was worried he might have passed it along to me.

The next day I woke up in exactly the same state. Practice wasn't much better—in fact it was almost exactly the same as the day before—and I again cut things short.

When I woke up on Friday, the symptoms had risen to a whole new level. Evan gave me the name and number of his ear, nose, and throat specialist, Dr. Mark Bianchi, and I went to meet him at St. Vincent's Hospital in Bridgeport. After a short exam, he determined that I was probably suffering from an ear infection and prescribed a stronger antibiotic. Because we were also headed into the weekend, he gave me his cell phone number, just in case.

As soon as I opened my eyes on Saturday morning, I knew something was seriously wrong: My head was beyond throbbing. I felt like somebody was going to work with a jackhammer in there, and my throat was so sore that when I swallowed I almost gagged from the pain. As it had been for the past two days, all of this only took place on the left side.

I sat up on the edge of the bed and took stock of my condition. I had always had a high threshold for pain, but this was a lot to bear. It hurt worse than anything I had ever felt, putting to shame the pain from my broken neck and the other injuries I've suffered throughout my career. Everything was pulsat-

Seeing as how my parents met playing tennis, it was clear pretty early on that I was going to be spending a lot of time on the court. (PHOTO COURTESY OF BETTY BLAKE)

All through his life my father exercised constantly. Here he is with me and Thomas in his classic warm-ups.
(PHOTO COURTESY OF BETTY BLAKE)

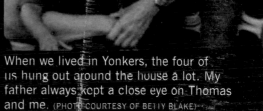

When we lived in Yonkers, the four of us hung out around the house a lot. My father always kept a close eye on Thomas and me. (PHOTO COURTESY OF BETTY BLAKE)

Growing up, my mom spent a ton of time with my brother and me. Whether we were living in Yonkers or in Fairfield, our home was always filled with joy. (PHOTO COURTESY OF BETTY BLAKE)

That's me in the front holding the trophy and Thomas on the right holding a plaque. Note that he's about twice my size. It took me a long time to catch up to him. (PHOTO COURTESY OF BETTY BLAKE)

When my brother went to Harvard to play tennis, I had a feeling that I wouldn't be far behind him. Two years later, I was playing there with him. (PHOTO COURTESY OF BETTY BLAKE)

This was taken at the French Open in 2002. The red clay of European courts has never been my favorite surface, and it was on clay like this two years later that I broke my neck. (PHOTO BY ART SEITZ)

The original J Block (PHOTO BY ART SEITZ)

After my first tournament win at Legg Mason tournament in Washington DC in 2002, it seemed like everything in my life was going to be perfect. (PHOTO BY ART SEITZ)

Here I'm with Todd Martin, my close friend and occasional mentor. It was Todd who first told me, "If you can win one set, you can win two." (PHOTO BY ART SEITZ)

Before my injuries I was constantly out on tour, but I made the most of my time at home with my friends. (PHOTO BY EVAN PAUSHTER)

With the constant traveling of the ATP, a real bond forms between many of the players. Here I am with Andy Roddick, Pete Sampras, NBA star Jason Kidd, and Andre Agassi.
(PHOTO BY EVAN PAUSHTER)

Going up for a slam at a charity event near Delray Beach, Florida. (PHOTO BY ART SEITZ)

Getting better is the only way to win. (PHOTO BY RON C. ANGLE)

Whenever they could, my parents would make it out to tournaments. Knowing that they were there supporting me always improved my play. (PHOTO BY ART SEITZ)

Through his entire life, my father read constantly—sometimes not even my tennis matches were enough to make him put a book down. (PHOTO BY EVAN PAUSHTER)

My best friend on the tour, Mardy Fish, making sure that my hair stays short.
(PHOTO BY RON C. ANGLE)

Before (PHOTO BY ART SEITZ)

After (PHOTO BY ART SEITZ)

My superman (PHOTO COURTESY OF BETTY BLAKE)

At the Legg Mason tournament in DC during the summer of 2005. I made it to the finals against Andy Roddick, which set me up perfectly for my run during the Pilot Pen and the US Open. (PHOTO BY RON C. ANGLE)

The J-Block was one of the best parts of my comeback. I never expected that kind of support, and it helped my tennis more than I ever could have imagined.
(© GETTY IMAGES/PILOT PEN TENNIS)

At the Pilot Pen in 2005. Fire it up one time. . . . Bam!

After winning in New Haven in 2005, I realized that with Brian's "getting better" plan, winning had become a whole lot easier. (© GETTY IMAGES/PILOT PEN TENNIS)

The J-Block finished the tournament right beside me. (PHOTO BY EVAN PAUSHTER)

My second-round match against Rafael Nadal during the 2005 US Open tested my limits, but it was there that I showed I was finally match tough.
(PHOTO BY RON C. ANGLE)

The quarterfinal match with Andre at the 2005 US Open was one of the most difficult of my career, but after that night I never doubted myself again. (PHOTO BY RON C. ANGLE)

Agassi 3 3 6 6 7
Blake 6 6 3 3 6

US OPEN

MassMutual

As Andre later said, the real winner that night was tennis. (PHOTO BY RON C. ANGLE)

In 2006, I played in the year-end Master's tournament in Shanghai. If you told me during the summer of 2004 that I'd be there two years later, I never would have believed you. (PHOTO BY RON C. ANGLE)

ing and firing, so much so that it was hard to shut it out and think.

Focus, James, c'mon, focus.

I had never felt as physically ill as I did just then. The only good thing about it was that I had completely forgotten about my rusty bicep.

Focus!

I played back the last two weeks in my mind: the specter of my father lying on his deathbed; the grass-court matches in Newport and my mother's grief-stricken face in the stands; my verge-of-tears eulogy at the funeral; and the weekend that had followed—a blur of hugs and tears and long walks and sleepless hours looking right up through the roof of my house and up into the heavens, right up at my father.

That must be it, I thought. The cumulative effect of grief, insomnia, and the exertion of my first matches in a few months had simply worn me down.

I went into the bathroom and looked into the mirror. There was a splotchy red rash with small, scaly blisters covering the skin on the top of my head and it ran down the left side of my neck.

I broke out in a cold sweat. What could possibly be going on? And as I stood there trying to calm myself down and analyze the situation, I was also aware of an odd sensation in my face—no, a *lack* of sensation.

I stood back to get a better look at myself and realized that the entire left side of my face wasn't moving, the skin seeming to droop a little the way it does on the face of some stroke victims.

I tried to blink my left eye. It didn't move.

I tried to force it.

Nothing.

Oh man. What is going on?

The entire left side of my face was paralyzed.

This is serious.

My breathing accelerated.

Easy, James. Take it easy. Slow it down. One step at a time.

I was alarmed and tried to stave off panic. There was a non-stop drumbeat in my head and I couldn't move my eye—it was lifeless and raw and dry as parchment, and I also realized for the first time that it burned. I pushed the lid closed with my finger and it stayed down, like a window shade, not opening again until I pushed it back up, the "blinking" activating the tear ducts and releasing some much-needed lubrication.

A tear streamed down my lifeless left cheek, the only sign that anything there was working at all.

I didn't know what to do or who to call. Thomas had gone off to play the qualifying rounds at the RCA Championships in Indianapolis, and Brian had gone along with him. My house-mates had taken off early to go to the beach. And there was no way I'd have called my mother just then, not after everything she'd just been through.

Some clouds parted in my mind and I remembered that cell phone number scribbled on a piece of paper in my wallet. I ran back upstairs, got it, and called Dr. Bianchi. He told me to meet him at the emergency room at St. Vincent's Hospital in Bridgeport.

I met Dr. Bianchi at the hospital and he had me admitted. Given what I'd just been through with my father and my neck, it was an all-too-familiar setting, but that did not make it any more comfortable. Having spent my fair share of time at hospitals, I'm not really sure there is such a thing as a comfortable one.

The admitting doctor ordered a number of tests: a CAT scan to rule out a brain tumor, blood tests, and on and on. She asked if I'd been under any unusual stress lately, and I laughed more than I had in a week.

"Yes," I said. "I suppose you could say I've been under some stress."

I kept my cool, but mentally I was plunged right back into that uncertain place I found myself in Rome, with no idea whatsoever what the implications of this crisis were. Was my comeback already over? Was my career about to be put in jeopardy *again*?

My other overriding thought was how to keep my mother

from finding out where I was. I could only imagine what it would do to her to discover I was in the hospital after the events of the past few weeks. As I was considering this, my cell phone rang, and I glanced down to see my mother's phone number in the caller ID window. I thought about letting it go to voice mail, then answered and decided to tell her the truth.

"But don't come over, Mom," I said. "You've seen enough hospitals the past few weeks."

She was there ten minutes later. She was, of course, a bit dazed, but remarkably didn't seem at all tired or stressed, and she stayed there and kept me company.

The next day, Dr. Bianchi gave me the test results.

"I don't think this is anything more than zoster," he told me. I didn't know what that meant. He explained that zoster, or shingles, is caused by the same virus that causes chicken pox, which I had when I was very young. If you don't completely knock out the virus, it can lay dormant for years. It usually doesn't act up, if ever, until the carrier is in his or her fifties or sixties, but it can be triggered by stress. In my case, the virus had caused a facial nerve to swell in its canal, cutting off the blood supply.

The diagnosis explained all my symptoms: the rash, the pain, the paralysis, the skewed taste in my mouth—they were all hallmarks of zoster. Dr. Bianchi was very honest with me, and he told me upfront that he had only treated one case of zoster before, so he was far from an expert. He said that he had little doubt that I *would* recover from this in time—although he was quick to point out that zoster could be unpredictable, and recovery could be a slow proposition marked by frustrating plateaus. His main concern was preserving the nerve, since there was a chance it could dry up like a desert creek, leaving my face paralyzed for good.

My brain did its usual filtering, focusing only on the positive news: that I would recover meant that I could play again. Paralyzed face? Whatever—so I'll wear sunglasses and a hat. Who cares? It seemed like a nonissue as long as I'd be able to recover and play.

Bianchi kept me in the hospital for about three days, for observation and to keep medicine flowing into my body by IV to really attack the virus as quickly as possible. Despite the bleak setting, it wasn't all that bad, though he couldn't do anything to fix the fact that I couldn't move half of my face. Word got out that I had been checked in, and friends began dropping by, like my old pal and juniors doubles partner, Matt Daly, who showed up, took one look at me, and burst out laughing.

"I'm sorry, man, but you look ridiculous," he said.

I had to laugh; at least as best I could with only half of a working face.

It was good to have my friends around during those days: one morning, on their way to work, Evan, Matt, and J.P., all of whom teach tennis, came over with decks of cards and poker chips, and we had a midmorning game right there in my room. It wasn't quite like sitting in my living room at home, but it felt pretty good for being in the hospital.

I was fast getting over my aversion to medication. Dr. Bianchi put me on a number of them, each one there for a specific task, such as prednisone, which would help reduce the swelling of the nerve. I also had to apply eye drops constantly (dry eyes are common with zoster, especially because you don't blink), and some ointment for my ear.

Over these days, I realized that although I was getting medicine into my bloodstream, the virus was still setting up camp. Another symptom of the infection was that it threw off my sense of balance, so I wobbled a little when I walked (imagine trying to walk a straight line after too many beers and you get the picture). Also the hearing in my left ear was diminished, like I had wads of cotton stuffed in there, so everything I heard on that side was muted. Yet another risk was that I was potentially contagious. Because zoster is caused by the same virus that causes chicken pox, I could give chicken pox to anyone who hadn't already had it.

For a few days, the meds and virus battled it out, and it seemed like the meds were winning. The left side of my face was still paralyzed, and my balance was off, but the rash was fading, and I was discharged on orders to continue taking meds, refrain from any physical activity for as long as I was taking them, and get lots of rest.

I was excited. I still felt very much under the weather, but I was already thinking about my next tournament. I had pulled out of Indy when the symptoms started, so I turned my focus to the Legg Mason tournament in Washington, DC, the week of August 16. What better place could there be to come back (again) than the site of my lone tournament victory two long years ago?

But just as I set my sights on this goal, something strange happened: my improvement hit a brick wall, just as Dr. Bianchi said it might. My face was still paralyzed, my balance was still off, the hearing wasn't coming back in my left ear, and water, and everything else I put in my mouth, still tasted funny, with a harsh, metallic aftertaste.

For the next three weeks, I pretty much stayed home. Dr. Bianchi forbade me from working out while on the medication, so I was back to my fractured-neck routine: playing poker with Evan, who was still recovering from tonsillitis and essentially passing the same twenty-dollar bill back and forth between us, watching *SportsCenter* and *Saturday Night Live* reruns (if I never see Jon Lovitz doing that pathological liar sketch again, it'll be too soon), and looking forward to my next meal.

Every day I'd leave the house to get lunch from Firehouse

or Chef's Table or some other local place. I looked like a guy taking a sobriety test as I did my tightrope walk into town, but it was one of the few things I had to look forward to in my everyday routine. When I'd get home, I'd savor each and every bite, dragging the meal on for as long as possible, almost glad for the facial paralysis because it forced me to move slowly.

The extreme boredom made it difficult to keep my thoughts from drifting to how much I missed my father, especially because I was drawing on his sterling example of how to be a model patient to guide me during this time. My recollections of him ran the gamut: some memories brought a smile to my face while others, sometimes just the thought of him and the fact that he was gone, left me softly crying in the midday seclusion of my living room. I used to think that crying was a sign of weakness, but not anymore—it was a valuable part of the healing process, helping my spirit recover from grief at the same time my body was recovering from illness.

As the weeks wore on, I wasn't just bored, I was beginning to physically break down. I was stiff and my back ached from the scoliosis, prompting me to get up and stretch it out every few hours, and the stretching made me wish I were getting ready to work out. Remembering how I had developed blisters when I headed back to Tampa in June, I began gripping my racket while sitting there watching television, trying to keep my calluses from fading again, but the frustration of not being able to swing it, not being able to move with it, began to take its toll.

For most of my life, I was used to getting naturally tired at night, having thoroughly exercised and pushed my body to its physical bounds during the day. But now, I'd find myself wide awake late into the night, staying up way past my housemates' bedtime. I was also dropping weight, because my muscles were beginning to atrophy and lose their mass. This annoyed the women in the house; I'd taunt them by telling them that no matter how much I ate I just couldn't keep the weight *on*.

But beneath the facade, I was beyond being frustrated—I was getting concerned. I called Dr. Bianchi, who reminded me that he really wasn't a specialist and put me in touch with Dr. John Kveton, a neurotologist who teaches at Yale.

Brian and I drove up to New Haven and met with Dr. Kveton. After an examination, we sat down in his office to discuss my status.

"How long could this take?" asked Brian.

"At least three months," Dr. Kveton said. "Or it could take four years."

Four years is a life sentence for a tennis player. The next day, Brian and I were talking and I told him that I hoped to get back on court in time for the US Open, which began in late August, just about a month away. Even after knowing me for more than a decade, his jaw dropped: "James, didn't you hear the doctor yesterday? It could take a lot longer than that."

"Nope," I said. "Didn't hear it."

Do I sound stubborn? Well, I guess maybe I am. *Definitely* am when it comes to somebody telling me that something's impossible. But there was another reason I chose to be so optimistic: my daily routine, if you could even call it a routine, was slowly driving me nuts. I had never been so inactive in my life. I could handle it with the neck injury because it came with an end-date, and of course it provided me all that time with my father. But Dr. Kveton's instruction was to be patient, to let the nerve in my face heal, millimeter by millimeter, until things got back to normal.

After about another week and a half, I couldn't take it any more. I decided to get back on the court. Brian was against it, reminding me of Dr. Kveton's advice. He tried to persuade me with a joke: "I don't want to hit with you James," he said. "You might get hurt, and if I beat you, what am I going to say? That I beat a guy with one working eye?"

I told him we'd take it easy, and convinced him to do it. Evan, who saw how low I was and thought I could at least use the workout, came along, and the three of us met one morning at Fairfield University. The two of them took their positions along the baseline on one side of the court, and I took the other side. Brian fed me a ball, I crouched slightly, took my racket back, and suddenly the ball was right there. I swung and sprayed it off to the court on my right.

Instantly, I realized just how many things were wrong. Not only was my balance off, but my vision was messed up as well—I had a hard time tracking the ball from Brian's and Evan's rackets to my own. I could see them hit it, I'd sort of lose it for a moment, then suddenly it would register much closer to me. This was especially disconcerting because neither Brian nor Evan hit anywhere near as hard as the average tour player. I ran to my right for a shot and realized that the vision impairment made even more of a difference in my coordination for running shots. Never before had I thought about the number of calculations that go on in the space of a nanosecond, enabling you to whack a ball on the run, but I was profoundly aware of them now.

"It's okay," Brian called out, supportive even though I had already confirmed that his hesitancy was well justified. "Here's another."

He hit another tennis ball my way and I overcompensated, sending it into the fence on the other side of the court.

It went on like this for a few minutes until I finally hit a ball back to them and decided to try some volleys at the net. I figured I'd have better luck if we took the bounce out of the equation, but after a couple of tries I realized my balance and coordination were so off-kilter that not only couldn't I hit the balls—the balls almost hit *me*.

It was a strange and sobering moment. Although shots are routinely sent my way at speeds of over a hundred miles per hour, I'd never been afraid on a tennis court. But now, I had to wonder, what if I was standing out there with a professional tennis player sending little fuzzy yellow-green missiles my way?

In search of a silver lining, I decided to hit some serves, the shot over which a player has the most control. Walking to the baseline, I bounced a ball a few times, tossed it up, and took a crack at it, delivering a sad, glancing blow that sent it off at a sharp angle.

It's virtually unheard of for a professional tennis player to mishit a serve; over the next few minutes I mishit one out of every three.

"That's it," I said. "I'm going home."

That was the first time when I really came to recognize the limits of willpower and resolve. I would have been happy to have come off the court with a good workout under my belt, but my shirt wasn't even damp. Frustrated and discouraged, I got in my car, drove home, turned on *Saturday Night Live*, and plopped on the sofa, and didn't laugh at all.

When I was eleven years old, my parents signed up Thomas and me for a weekly shared, half-hour lesson at the local club in nearby Trumbull, Connecticut. The lessons were with the owner, Ed Pagano.

By then my brother and I were both good players, but I found tennis to be very frustrating, and not just in competition. A poorly timed forehand would tick me off so badly that I'd fire the next ball into the wall or the ceiling. It was precisely the kind of thing that I never would have done in front of my father, and though Ed Pagano was far from being my father, it was pretty clear that he didn't want me to do it in front of him either.

Mr. Pagano was getting up there in years, and I guess he felt that he didn't need this kind of behavior in his life, so when a young local professional player named Brian Barker came back to the area and became a pro at the club, one of the first jobs Mr. Pagano gave him was to take over the Blake brothers' lesson. A former top one hundred college player, and number one New England junior player before that, Brian had just completed a six-month stretch of professional play. Needless to say, dealing with two preteens, one of whom frequently displayed a nasty temper, was not high on his list of choice assignments. I can still remember the first day we were hitting and I was throwing a fit when Mr. Pagano walked by.

"Thanks a lot, Ed," Brian said, affecting a perfect deadpan. "This is great."

Within a year or so, Thomas and I graduated to having

individual lessons. Now that I didn't have to worry about ruining Thomas's time, I really let my temper fly, stomping around and slamming balls whenever I felt the least bit frustrated.

Brian absorbed this for a while with near-saintly patience, but then he decided to speak up.

"Okay. Okay. Okay," Brian said. He let his racket fall to his side and walked over to the net. "Come here."

What was this? I wondered. Why wasn't he just feeding me another ball?

"No," I said. "Let's keep hitting. C'mon. Hit me another."

"It's okay. Come here."

I had no idea what was coming. I slowly, almost suspiciously, walked up to the net.

"James. Why are you getting so upset? You can't get every forehand right."

"There's no reason to miss an easy forehand," I said, looking down at my shoes. I didn't want to talk. I wanted to get back to the baseline and hit some more balls.

"Everyone misses forehands," he said. "It's part of the game."

He motioned me over to the side of the court and we sat down on the bench.

"What's going on with you?"

This was getting weird. What was going on with me? What

did this guy care what was going on with me? I was there to hit, not talk.

"What do you mean?"

"What's going on with your life? Are you happy?"

"Yeah, sure," I said.

There are people, many of them, who play at the Tennis Club of Trumbull, who refer to what I was engaging in as a "Barker lesson": five minutes of hitting, followed by twenty-five minutes of talking. As I would come to learn, Brian's something of a philosopher-coach who has many strongly held beliefs about the relationship between tennis and life. If there's something wrong in your life, it'll show in your tennis game—not always in predictable ways, but in ways that are logical: self-belief might be manifested in weak second serves, impatience can cause you to make low-percentage gambles, and so on.

I wasn't at all into the idea of squandering my precious half hour on the sidelines, talking about the life that was waiting for me outside the club—I wanted to *play*. I left that day shaking my head, not really sure about what had transpired or why and wondering if maybe we should be thinking of switching to one of the other pros at the club.

But when I showed up the next week, I was a bit more patient. Oh, my tantrums came, but at least I *thought* about them before they did, and the more talking we did, the more patient I got.

One day, my mother came to pick me up, and the mother of another boy who took lessons with Brian pulled her aside. "You know, I pay a lot of money for these lessons," the woman said. "And all they do is stand there and talk."

"That's okay," my mom replied, a firm believer in the value of Brian's approach. When she told me about it, I said, "Her son is getting more out of that than hitting balls."

In competition, I would still get angry on the court all the time—everyone who played in the New England juniors has a story about playing me or watching me play during a match in which I flew into a ridiculous rage. Evan can tell you about the time I hurled my racket over the fence into the next court, *where there was a match going on.* My mother will tell you about the time I lost to a guy with a Mohawk and spent the drive home mangling a pen and repeating, over and over, "I lost to a guy . . . in a *Mohawk.*"

But while my anger seemed intricately linked to my losses, it quickly became apparent that I had been thinking about winning, tennis, and life, using the wrong set of objectives. All my anger and frustration came from my desire to win, my wanting to get to the next level, but I couldn't focus on how I would achieve this. When I felt like I was experiencing a setback, I lost all my focus and just got mad. It was very similar to what I went through in 2003, only as a professional I kept my frustration during matches bottled up; but when I was teenager, I let everything, all my disappointment and anger, come pouring out.

Gradually, during my training with Brian, he began to instill in my teenage mind an idea that I would never have come to on my own: "Don't worry about winning every match or about your regional ranking—just worry about getting better."

From that moment on, getting better became the focus of all my energy. Brian and I obsessed over it during our hours talking on the bench; it was such a simple concept, and yet it had such a far-reaching application. First and foremost, it put success in my hands, because I was the one who was defining what success meant to me. If getting better was the definition of success, then as long as I was getting better, I was succeeding. Brian told me that there were things that would happen in life that I wouldn't be able to control—I might get injured, or come up against guys who were just better than I was, or maybe I'd never grow tall, which was a concern in those shrimpy days of mine.

The ultimate thing that was out of my control was my level of talent, and just getting better also made that an easier pill to swallow. If the best I could do was to get a college scholarship and never make it on the pro tour, I'd have been able to live with that, so long as I had done my best to get there.

Part of the reason that I took so naturally to Brian's philosophy was that it fit so perfectly with how my father had raised me. Like Brian, my father believed that the focus should be on improvement—not victory—and he believed that hard work was the *only* way to achieve that. He was always trying to instill this discipline in others. He volunteered at the Harlem Junior Tennis Program, where kids would show up to play tennis and find that their day began with calisthenics.

"You're getting better today," my father would tell them, then lead them in sit-ups, push-ups, leg lifts, and a jog around the armory. At first a lot of the kids complained, but I've heard stories of their coming back, years later, and reporting how he had inspired them.

Where my father differed from Brian was that he believed in setting goals, very specific goals, to help ensure follow through. But my father—though set in his ways—also had the capacity to change, and in time, after many long debates with Brian, he came to believe, or at least accept, that tennis was different, that maybe you couldn't set the same kind of goals in tennis as you could in academics or business.

These values of my father and my coach became a rhythmic presence in my brain: *Work hard, get better. Work hard, get better. Work hard, get better.*

I heard this refrain all the time, and I pushed myself from even a very young age: in the morning, before school, I'd go hit with my brother.

Work hard, get better. Work hard, get better.

During my junior and senior years of high school, when I

had a certain amount of freedom to set my class schedule, I always tried to keep the last period of the day free so I could get to the courts before the rest of the team. I'd either hit with the ball machine or just take a hopper full of balls and practice serving, whatever I could think of on a given day. I just wanted work to do.

Work hard, get better.

One day, I was playing a set against Evan, and he couldn't help but notice that my game had come up a notch in a very short time: I was chasing down more balls, hitting my forehand with more authority, and not getting tired.

"What have you been doing?" he asked.

"Working hard, Ev," I said, smiling the same smile I had seen my father smile so many times. "Just working hard, that's all."

———

In early August, I decided to try to hit again. I called Brian and we met at the courts at Fairfield University. It wasn't a great practice, but it was a lot better than the last one. Brian hit a lot of balls right to me, and I was able to keep them in the court. Plus it felt so good just to be out there again, running and hitting. It felt good to have sweat running down my face and soaking into my shirt. It felt good to be *outside.*

There was a limit to how much I could play, so Brian and I

returned to our old tradition of a decade earlier: sitting on the sidelines and talking. And just like when I was a kid, I got as much out of the talks as I did from the tennis. We talked about my dad and about how much we both missed him. We talked about how much pressure I put on myself and what the good and bad aspects of that were. We talked about how important it was to be a good person and about how much that meant to both of us, even more than the tennis meant. A devout Catholic, Brian also talked about my father, about how he was sure he was in heaven, and about how he knew he'd be proud of me. Coming from him, that meant a lot. Brian also tried to make me feel better about my condition, announcing little signs of improvement, like when he thought the left side of my face was beginning to move a little.

In addition, we returned to the idea of getting better, discussing whether or not I was going to be able to return stronger than I was before. As Brian and I continued to practice and talk, it was clear that I wasn't playing my best, but I rationalized it with the notion that it had been weeks since I had hit. The medication, I told myself, was throwing me off.

Against my better judgment, I decided to play the Legg Mason tournament in Washington, DC, the week of August 16. Brian and I both knew I wasn't ready—in addition to my zoster-related problems, I had developed a blister on my hand in practice and had also pulled a stomach muscle that week—but we thought it'd be a good way to gauge whether I should play the US Open.

It was worth going to DC just to see some of the other guys for the first time in months. I had an especially funny run-in with Mardy Fish and Robby Ginepri. Mardy had clearly decided that he wasn't going to make a big deal about my droopy, immobile face, except to poke fun at it and make me laugh. As the three of us were hanging out and catching up, whenever I cracked a half smile, he'd push the left side of my mouth up to set things right.

My first-round match was scheduled for a Wednesday night, August 18, and I was second up, after Andre Agassi and Paul Goldstein, two of the guys I really missed while I was away. They were happy to see me, but neither of them really knew what was going on, beyond the fact that my face looked mangled.

I came out of the tunnel onto the court that night, and right away I knew I had made a mistake. The glare of the lights was something that neither I nor Brian had factored into our thinking. I had to squint just to walk out to my chair, drop off my bag, and get to the net for the coin toss. When my name was announced it was completely anticlimactic, and I had the most ominous sense of déjà vu that took me back to Newport. All of a sudden there was no joy in being there.

During the warm-up alone, my worst fears were confirmed.

I couldn't do anything right: my serves had no pop on them, my ground strokes lacked purpose or accuracy, and before the first point was event played, my confidence began to wane. Rather than feeling like I was about to play a tennis match, I felt like I was about to get into a boxing ring with somebody in a higher weight class. Even though my opponent, a Chilean named Adrian Garcia, was a few inches shorter than I was, and hardly an imposing presence on the court, I felt like I was about to get my ass kicked.

The first set flew by in a shot. I lost it 1–6.

Up in the box, Brian and Thomas looked on with despair, but their presence was comforting, since they were the only two people there who knew what I was going through.

I kept trying to find a way to win, or at least to win some games. At one point I decided to try beating him with my legs, chipping all his shots back in hopes of tiring him out or frustrating him. When that didn't work, I began ripping the ball, going for broke with my forehand, but he patiently blocked them back, one after the other, until I went for too much and missed wide.

I looked over to my side: sitting shoulder to shoulder with the photographers on a courtside bench were a group of supervisors from the ATP, barely able to conceal their shock at what was transpiring.

But the worst part of the evening was the fans, who kept trying to urge me on right through to the bitter end. Not only was I the crowd favorite based on patriotism, but I had also had a lot of success here. The fans were doing everything in their power to propel me onward, but their efforts were wasted. I hadn't ever been so discouraged during a match. Usually I feel like there's *something* I can do to turn things around when they get bad, but that night I knew that unless Mr. Garcia developed a sudden case of food poisoning, I was going to be the one with an *L* in his results column at the end of the night. That's exactly what happened.

I got home and the next day I pulled out of the US Open.

That tournament was a frustrating benchmark in what long ago had become a frustrating summer. The moment I had been anticipating for weeks—that first return to tournament play in front of fans—now seemed more like a fantasy than an eventuality, because my first attempt to realize it had been such a public embarrassment.

I was getting more and more despondent, but I found a source of strength in the most unlikely of places. Not long after the day when I discovered the signs of zoster on my face, I began a daily ritual of scrutinizing myself in the mirror to see if I could detect any movement on the left side of my face. I've never spent much time looking in the mirror, but since even the slightest sign of improvement would give me a great deal of hope, I began looking religiously. I'd smile and survey the left side of my lips to see if they turned up when I moved my mouth.

As my habit of looking in the mirror took hold, I began to find something else about my appearance: though I'd never really noticed it before, I'd come to look a lot like my father. This hadn't always been especially apparent, but looking in the mirror and studying my reflection, it was obvious that with my shaved head I had a strong physical resemblance to him—especially during stretches when I let my beard grow in.

I didn't come to see this in a single, sudden moment; it was something that happened through time, through my ritual of caring for that other half of my face. The more I looked, the more I saw him there, staring back at me. My reflection had become his, a daily reminder of his sterling example and the work that I still had to do. When I said those words at my father's funeral about finding a way to make him live forever, I could never have imagined that I would take such direct inspiration from him just a few weeks later—here I was, a patient just like he was, laid up at home, just like he was. In many ways, my life during those weeks had come to reflect his time at home, and his example taught me how to behave with dignity during times far worse than what I was dealing with. Our reflections, which had always been close, were now inextricably intertwined, and so with him in mind, I kept myself positive during those weeks— weeks when, in retrospect, I didn't have much to be positive about.

I continued to see Dr. Kveton and to visit Dr. Bianchi.

They'd monitor how well the medications were working and test my hearing, and Bianchi would drain my ear, a disgusting spectacle, about which I'll spare you the details.

I was really disappointed to miss the Open, but there were a few happy memories I associate with it. On the Sunday before the tournament kicked off, I decided to participate in Arthur Ashe Kids' Day, a family-geared afternoon of musical performances, clinics, and other events that is always a lot of fun. I didn't really feel like I belonged there with active players like Andre Agassi, and I was worried that I might embarrass myself by totally missing the ball during one of the clinics. Complicating matters further was that I had made it a point not to let anyone photograph me during this time, but I knew the event would be televised. In truth, it was a gamble for a number of reasons, but I didn't know if I'd ever have a chance to play at Ashe Stadium, or any stadium, again, so I put on some shades and went. I was glad I did because it was a welcome opportunity to enjoy some of the most wonderful aspects of being a professional player, interacting with the fans—it wasn't in the context of a match, but it was the next best thing.

The other place when people managed to get me in front of the camera was during the Open, when I hooked up with Mardy Fish and Robby Ginepri for dinner in New York City. Mardy took a picture of me on his cell phone and kept laughing at it, and periodically throughout the evening, he'd slap the side of my face that was paralyzed and say, "Can you feel that?" Of course I could, but he did it over and over until it became hilarious.

I followed the Open on television, noteworthy largely for how Roger Federer followed up his second Wimbledon win with his first title in New York. It was fast becoming clear how much of a force he was turning into, especially since, in the final, he took two of his three sets from Lleyton Hewitt at love.

Just a week after that, I decided to play a small tournament in Delray Beach, Florida. I knew I wasn't really good enough, but I was just so bored and wanted to be out with the guys again. My first match was against a local wild card who took the first set off me, but seemed overwhelmed by the occasion. He had a big first serve, but once the ball was in play, he could barely keep it inside the lines. I won in three.

After the match, Mardy found me and high-fived me.

"You're back!" he said, and his coach at the time, Kelly Jones, echoed the sentiment.

I knew they were wrong.

In the next round I played Vince Spadea, a bit of a character on the men's tour who's known almost as much for his amateur rapping ("Spadea ain't afraid-a ya" is his signature line) as he is for his tennis. Vince took the first set off me pretty handily, and once again, defeat seemed to be on the horizon.

But I kept on fighting, and I finally had my first positive moment on a court in months when I earned a break point in the second set. During the next point, Vince hit a weak ground stroke and my eyes opened wide. This was the moment I'd been waiting for, and I charged for it, ready to pound a running cross-court forehand . . .

. . . and totally wiffed, just missed the ball entirely. It sailed right past me and into the hands of a ball kid along the back fence.

I looked up at Brian and Mardy, put my hands on my hips, and started to laugh. Before long, it was all over. Vince and I shook hands, and I was out of the tournament and on my way home.

When we got back up North, Brian and I went to see Dr. Kveton, who told me to write off the rest of the tennis year. He meant that I should give up the year, *at a minimum*—skipping the indoor season in Europe and the Far East—and take stock in January, but I took it to mean that I should shoot for a return to action right after the New Year.

Even if I were right, that still meant I had another four months to kill before my next professional match. Guys had taken off less time than that and never fully regained their form or their careers. I was going to do my best to get mine back, but there were few guarantees that I would be successful.

Only time—*a lot* of time—would tell.

FIVE

PLAN B

SEPTEMBER–DECEMBER 2004

> I cannot help but think that childhood friends
> are the bedrock of all one's future relation-
> ships, and that you move away from them at
> your risk. There is an African proverb in which I
> believe: Hold on to your friends with both
> hands.
>
> —ARTHUR ASHE, *DAYS OF GRACE*

Brian Barker, my good friend, tennis mentor, and the great philosopher-coach of Fairfield County, likes to tell people that "if James thought hitting forehands for ten hours a day would make his forehand one percent better, then he'd hit forehands for ten hours a day."

He's not kidding. Hard work is almost a religion for me because, in many ways, it's the window through which I look for the answers to life's questions. Although my father's death and then my own medical crisis had shown me firsthand that there were some things even hard work could not overcome, I still believed that, in the end, it would be my salvation from everything that life had thrown at me over the past few months.

When Dr. Kveton told me to write off the tennis year, part of me found it to be a relief. Mentally, I was almost incapable of realizing that there was something wrong that willpower alone wasn't going to right, but my body could feel the truth of the situation. I never would have thrown in the towel myself, but under the banner "Doctor's Orders," I could live with it.

And yet, another part of me knew that, ironically, Dr. Kveton's advice presented one of the biggest challenges I'd ever taken on. The hardest things to do are those things that go against our own instincts, and by that measure, *not* working hard was actually going to be incredibly hard work for me. Sitting in his office, I already felt the walls closing in as I imagined another four months with no tournament play.

But there was no other choice; I'd have to put my faith in something that went against my father's teachings, against my own experience, against my very *nature*, and let nature itself do its work in healing me.

I'd also have to find ways to fill all that time.

———

Unless you're a pretty serious tennis fan, you probably don't know much about my coach, because Brian doesn't run around trying to elbow his way into the spotlight, writing books or even giving many interviews. Part of this is strategy; he doesn't feel anyone needs to know what we're talking about or working on. But most of it is him just being his exceedingly humble self.

From the first time he waved me up to the net for one of his patented talks, it's been clear to me that Brian knew and cared about me, but not necessarily in that order. He cared about me the way he cared about all his students, and eventually he came to know me. By the time I was thirteen, I considered him a friend, though I of course realize now that he had more to offer me than I could have possibly offered him back then. Nevertheless, we'd hook up for golf once in a while or to catch up over lunch.

There are definitely celebrity coaches in tennis, just as there are in any sport, but at a certain level, as far as I'm concerned, any smart coach is more or less just as good as any other smart coach. To me, the things you get from a coach off the court are just as, if not more, important than the advice they give you on the court—as Brian began teaching me when I was a little kid, what goes on inside those lines is largely a reflection of what goes on outside them.

In hindsight, Brian's comprehensive understanding of me helped save me that summer. While I could never have admitted it at the time, it was invaluable to have him objecting to my getting back out on tour prematurely, to remind me of the things that I let myself forget the doctors had said.

And so I shouldn't have been surprised that Dr. Kveton's recommendation to sideline me for the rest of the year provided Brian with yet another chance to fill this unenviable role.

"You know what, James," he told me in the car on the drive back to Fairfield. "We're only going to practice every other day for a while. You should take advantage of this time. Have some fun."

Have some fun?

As an end, fun had never been a priority for me. The thing that's always been the most fun for me was making progress and getting better; I wasn't entirely sure how to have fun for fun's sake. I decided to meet Brian halfway and indulge my need to impose my will on the situation, while staying fit for what was shaping up as a nearly yearlong off-season. I worked out every day, mostly on a stationery bike at the gym, although I would occasionally run outdoors, but we only practiced together every other day.

As for what to do with the rest of my time, much as I loved poker, I decided I should get out of the house and mix it up a bit. I went to Colorado for a few days to visit Thomas, who was there with a girl he was dating at the time. I went to Boston with a group of friends to see Gavin DeGraw perform. I headed down to Tampa to catch some Bucs games, and one weekend, Brian, Matt Daly, and Brian's pal Bobby Dzurenda (whom we all call Bobby D.) came down and we had ourselves a little competition weekend: golf, bowling, darts, pool, and anything else we could think of.

When I wasn't traveling, I spent time with people I didn't get to see very often, like my paternal grandfather who visited quite often from New York City. He had lost his wife and his son in the space of a year, so I was glad I could be there for him, though like my father, he never seemed to need a shoulder to cry on.

This time was valuable in and of itself, but it was also valuable because Brian was right: it was a frustrating grind on the court. I wasn't in pain any longer, and there was no rash on my face, although the left side remained somewhat paralyzed, but I was still very much in the grip of the virus, which was hard to gauge from day to day. One day we'd have an exceptional practice, the next I'd be misfiring balls and struggling to keep my balance and stay positive.

All through this, Brian was there, offering support wherever he could, but also serving as a force that kept me grounded and rational. I found myself thinking back to how Brian had helped me overcome my frustration as a little boy, and I realized if he had not taken the time to help train my anger out of me, I might not have been able to make it through this rough patch. I have him to thank for teaching me not only the mechanics of the game, but also the mechanics of myself. If my temper had gone unchecked in those younger days, I can only imagine how frustrated I'd have been that fall.

Many of the most difficult times came when Brian and I began to discuss the worst-case scenario spelled out by Dr. Kveton. I struggled to tolerate the thought that if the zoster lingered for a year or more, it might be the thing that brought my career to an end. But as that fall unfolded, I did more than tolerate those thoughts; I lived with them day and night. They practically moved into my house. And the reason I was able to cope in this way was Brian, who more than ever kept me focused on the positives. He'd remind me of how much I'd achieved and how hard I'd worked to achieve it. He'd remind me to feel good about what I'd had the opportunity to do. And he'd remind me that if there was even the slightest chance to get back to where I'd been before, that we'd go after it, heart and soul, together.

When I play tennis, my goal is to play *my* game, on my terms. But there are days when things aren't going your way, either because your opponent is playing too well, or you're a little off, or it's windy, or whatever. Those are the times when you have to go to Plan B, adjusting your idealized version of yourself to deal with the reality in front of you and, one hopes, come out on top.

In the early fall of that year, I learned that, in this way, life is no different than a tennis match. I thought about what it meant to lose your serve in tennis. There are three ways to lose your serve: one is that you can play poor points. Another is that you just serve weakly, timidly, allowing your opponent to tee off on his returns, taking control of the points, moving you to the sides and robbing those points that are supposed to belong to you.

If you do either of those, you have only yourself to blame.

The final way to lose serve is to be overwhelmed by an opponent, to find yourself on the receiving end of a barrage of brilliant returns backed up by power, aggression, and unpredictability. Instead of dictating play, you're scrambling all over the place, just trying to keep the ball in the court. Maybe there's even some plain bad luck—you break a string at a critical moment or a ball clips the top of the net and dribbles over to your side, hopelessly out of reach. Before you know it, you've lost four points and the game along with it.

In other words, it's possible to do nothing wrong and still lose your serve.

Anyone can have their serve broken that way, and when I look back on 2004, I feel like that's what happened to me—a freak accident on the tennis court, the loss of my father, the onset of a rare viral condition—an overwhelming onslaught of bad luck, bad news, and bad health.

As I went through my routine during the fall of 2004, I realized that I was learning in life the same lessons I needed to learn on the court back in 2003. When you're down, you have to be patient and take it one step at a time, to work your way back into the match.

This was a useful thought to have in the back of my mind as I slowly began to practice again. I just keep telling myself that breaking back in life, as in tennis, demands discipline—not desperation. I remembered my father's refrain, uttered to me since the time I was a little boy: *You can't control your ability, but you can control your level of effort.* If it turned out that the zoster had diminished my ability, I resolved that I'd work hard enough to stay on the tour. Maybe with the right effort level I could stay in the top hundred. Sure, I'd lose some endorsement money, and most likely, I would not win another title. But I'd continue to be able to travel, to be with my friends on the road, and to play matches in front of appreciative fans.

There was, of course, another Plan B, the one in which I imagined myself leaving the life of a professional athlete behind altogether. I thought about the possibility all too frequently, and like any professional athlete, I often visualized how my decision to end my career would play out on *SportsCenter.* The fact that I had never been on *SportsCenter* was irrelevant; I had the whole thing shot, edited, and scored in my head. I could hear the dramatic swell of the music and the voice over of the host telling my backstory. I could see myself moving in slow motion across the court as they rehashed old footage of me in my prime. I could see myself sitting in business-casual clothes in the television studio talking about the decision to leave and how satisfied I was with my choice, how I got to see my mom more now, how I still played for fun against my brother. I would smile and they would cut away to clips of me in my new life—perhaps working for some sort of sports marketing firm. I would beam with convincing satisfaction, flash a huge smile, and the piece would fade to black.

I honestly believe that if I couldn't have gotten back on my tennis feet, that I'd have been just as happy as I seemed in that imaginary profile piece, because it wasn't that long ago that I was embarking on a life not unlike the one depicted there.

When I was growing up, a "normal" life was all my family and I had ever envisioned for me, or for Thomas. Though my brother and I both had some tennis ability, we never considered going to one of the big academies, where a lot of today's top players spend their teenage years. The truth of the matter is that I wasn't good enough to have been recruited in my midteens, and beyond that, we were such a tight family that for one of us to be sent away would have been unthinkable. What's more, the twenty thousand dollars plus per year it would have cost was well beyond what my parents would have considered spending on tennis. We had a comfortable lifestyle, but it would have been a stretch and a strain to come up with that kind of funding. For college, they wouldn't have hesitated—they probably would have even sold their house if they had to—but for tennis, no way.

When I look back on my teenage years, I'm so thankful that I didn't go to a tennis academy. For one thing, I think I would have burned out on the sport, especially when I see how single-mindedly I pursue it now. For another, I wanted to have a traditional childhood, with school in the morning and tennis in the afternoon and on the weekend. I wanted to pass notes in class, hang out with my friends at lunch, and go to the prom. I also wanted to have a complete education and to do my parents proud by excelling in school—especially since that was always the most important thing in the world to them.

Another part of my "normal" childhood was playing on the Fairfield High School Tennis Team. It was all but unheard of for someone who played in the juniors to also play on their school team, and a lot of guys I met on the road thought I was crazy when they heard I did this, but I treasured the experience, and was (and still am) fond of my school's coach, John Honey.

Unlike my tennis academy counterparts on the tour, I had not been groomed to turn pro, and as such, it was not until the summer after my freshman year of college that I even started contemplating professional tennis. When my sophomore year began in the fall, I declared economics as my "concentration"

(Harvard-speak for "major"), mostly because I thought it would be the least time-consuming—fewer long essays to write, and shorter books to read. I wanted the lighter academic workload to see how I would do if I really pushed myself in training. My dorm that year was right on the Charles River, so I'd run along the river in the morning or go to the courts and ask one of the coaches to feed me balls for an extra hour. I also stayed after practice to work out with the strength coach, a great resource that most of the guys didn't take advantage of.

The effort paid off. My year got off to an awesome start, and I became the number one ranked college player. During the winter break, I played a Futures event (tennis's equivalent of the minor leagues, Futures events and the more valuable, prestigious Challenger tournaments offer opportunities for players to earn rankings points, and money, outside tour-level competition) in Altamonte Springs, Florida, and won the title. When I came back to Fairfield, I found myself believing for the first time that I might be good enough to turn pro. I began talking it over with my mother, my father, Thomas, and Brian—a number of ongoing and crisscrossing dialogues that would continue for months.

Over the course of these discussions, my parents made it quite obvious that they were still firmly rooted in the idea of a more normal path for me and my education. There was a lot that I stood to gain from staying in school, a fact that my parents chose to reinforce every time the subject of professional tennis came up. I have to say, it was a very hard point for me to argue against.

However, despite their preferences, some aspects of the situation were indisputable. My results had caught the attention of a number of sports agencies, and representatives from Advantage International (now called Octagon) and ProServ (which has since been acquired by SFX) began to court me, either tracking me down at school or calling my parents' house, where my father did his best to scare them off and keep them from derailing my college plans. In addition to those agencies, a few independent agents, such as rapper Master P, who at the time had a company called No Limit Sports, courted me. I guess they saw some crossover appeal in an African American tennis player, because I'm sure they weren't going after many other guys who played my sport.

With my parents participating in their subtly protective way, I began meeting with a few of these agents, often in Boston. Each of them would sell me on the relative merits of his or her agency. I was only two years removed from the college recruitment process and it all felt very familiar, with the added element of trying to determine whom I could trust. Having seen fictional characters in movies like *Jerry Maguire*, I was on the lookout for anything that seemed slick or distrustful or just plain too good to be true.

Part of my indecision was due to the fact that because I hadn't been raised to become a professional player, I didn't have any friends who had gone through the same process to call on for advice, so I had to figure it out as I went along. My one resource was Mats Wilander, the seven-time Grand Slam champ, who was friendly with Brian, and who had hit with me for the first time when I was fourteen, and had become a friend and advisor over the years. But while Mats could help point me in the right direction about people and places, there were still a lot of question marks that hung in the air.

Fortunately, there was another potential agent in the mix, one who had made a favorable impression on us a few years earlier—Carlos Fleming, a young, soft-spoken African American guy from IMG who had introduced himself to my father at the US Open junior tournament in 1997.

"Mr. Blake," he said after locating my father in the crowd during one of my matches, "I know that James is going to Harvard and that that's important to you. But when the time is right, I'm going to give you a call."

During my sophomore year, he called my father, who chuckled as he let Carlos know how important it was to him that people keep their word: "You said you'd call," he said, "and I believed you. I just didn't think it'd take almost two years."

A meeting was set in Boston. My parents drove up and Carlos met us all for breakfast. Because at the time he was a freshly minted agent, he was accompanied by Bill Ryan, a more seasoned IMG representative, who came with Mats' seal of approval. Unlike some of the other agents I'd been meeting with who painted the rosiest picture imaginable and told me all the things they could do for me, Bill was much more direct and realistic. "We can do these things for you," he said, *"if you deliver.* If you go out and get beat week after week, then we're not going to be able to do a whole lot for you."

I respected that honesty, and I think my father did, too.

Later that morning, my parents, Carlos, and Bill watched me practice. My father pulled Carlos aside for a brief heart-to-heart talk. "I just want you to know that we like you," he said. "But *we* will decide when James does or doesn't leave school."

Carlos smiled.

"What's so funny?" my father asked, wondering if his stern declaration was having the desired impact.

"My father would say the exact same thing, Mr. Blake."

As the year wore on, I won two of the collegiate "Grand Slams," including the All-Americans, in which I won singles and doubles, playing with Kunj Majmudar. The schedule there was pushed back due to rain, and I had to play two singles matches and two doubles matches in one day—which was probably the highlight of my year. At the end of the year, I made the finals of the NCAAs, where I lost to Jeff Morrison, but I held the number one ranking by enough of a margin that I kept it at year's end.

I teetered on the brink of my decision for the entire year, talking to some of those agents, especially Carlos, and to my parents and my brother. In the end, it was Thomas who got me over the hump. He was visiting me one night in the spring and we got to talking about it again. He just came out and said that he thought I couldn't get much better at the college level, and that he thought I was good enough to at least to make a go of it.

It was a validation of what I was thinking myself: Who knew how far I'd get? The worst case scenario was that I could always come back to Harvard—not exactly a bad Plan B.

The only person left to convince was the most important person: my father.

I had kept in good touch with Carlos, and right after the school year ended, I got in touch again and we had had a few more meetings. Carlos began talking to potential sponsors and managed to generate a lot of interest in me. He was trying to line up a deal that would make it possible for me to leave school with an insurance policy of some kind.

The solution Carlos came up with was perfect: with a strong ally in Nike's scout Jim Tressler, who was impressed by my performance at the NCAAs, he convinced Nike to pony up a signing bonus, which is all but unheard of. When he got them to agree to it, he called my father and made his pitch. With the money he had lined up, I could leave school, and if things didn't work out, I could return with all the remaining tuition in my back pocket.

Despite his belief in the importance of education, when he heard this news from Carlos, my father did a complete one-eighty on the subject of my turning pro. It must have been hard for him, but he saw what I wanted and that I could do it responsibly.

He gave me his blessing: "I want you to keep working hard," he told me. "This is something I want you to be successful at."

I gave him my word, and with that, the last tumbler had fallen into place: I decided to go pro.

———————

I thought a lot about those college days in the fall of 2004, about driving to and from Boston and playing college tennis and declaring a concentration—feeling a bit nostalgic for what were very good times. I began to imagine not just Plan Bs for the future, but also Plan Bs for the past, roads that I might have taken instead of the one I chose.

As I looked back on my time at Harvard, I came to realize that it wouldn't have taken much to have kept me in college and on a more conventional career path. All it would have required was a few more losses or not meeting an agent like Carlos. Without the victories, I wouldn't have had the interest, without Carlos I wouldn't have had my father's approval. Failure on either of these fronts would have kept me right where I was, but as fate would have it, that's not how it worked out.

During these months at home in the fall of 2004, I had a chance to see what "normal" life was like, the "real life" that most professional athletes never get to experience. Of course, I had experienced glimpses of it during my short stays in town, but those were always whirlwind visits and often at the holidays when nobody else is working either. Though technically I had been living a "normal" existence since I broke my neck, it was not until Dr. Kveton revoked the remainder of my tennis season that I started to see myself assimilating into anything that seemed like a "normal" routine.

Before everything happened, I had previously had a tough time relating to certain aspects of my friends' lives. I loved them all just the same, but because the routine of my life deviated so sharply from theirs, it was not always easy for me to put myself in their shoes. I was often a silent participant in conversations about work, commuting, and so on—the everyday stuff that most people in the world discuss.

Living in the house with my friends while I was sick, I would have breakfast with them in the morning, then spend most of the day alone. By dinnertime, I was eagerly awaiting the moment when I'd hear cars pulling up in the driveway and the front door opening. Often my reaction was downright Pavlovian, running to the front door at the sound of the key turning to greet whoever might be on the other side. Whereas my life had previously been one long weekend, I now looked forward to the *actual* weekend, because that's when my friends were off from work and we could hang out together all day.

My friends really helped me in those days: I didn't talk about it much, but I was very self-conscious about the nonfunctional side of my face, and they'd encourage me to come out with them, lobbying hard for me to get off the couch and enjoy a night roaming the bars on Post Road. I think it helped me recover, people making me feel better all the time and making me smile, even if it was only a half smile. In addition to my housemates and the usual gang who came by at night, I began to get visits from a lot of other friends, even people I hadn't seen in a long while, who had heard I was sick and showed up at my door with a card or a home-cooked meal and would sit and visit with me for a few hours.

Spending all that time with my friends threw one of my earliest decisions about my professional career into greater focus. In November 1999, a few months after turning pro, I won Futures events in Haines City, Florida, and Clearwater, Florida, then began playing nothing but Challenger events, with an occasional wildcard into a tour-level tournament. I reached the quarterfinals in my next Challenger event, then, for almost a year, failed to win more than two matches in a row. It was a very humbling, frustrating time, and a lot of guys in my position—

suffering early-round losses over and over—would have begun to travel the world in search of rankings points, going all the way to Challenger events in places as remote as India, Vietnam, or Uzbekistan to exploit the weak field and come back with a higher ranking. But I decided against that, opting instead to stay here in the States where my brother was with me, which meant we could also play doubles a lot, and I was able to sneak off to Connecticut once in a while. It was a huge decision for me because it set the tone for everything else about my career and established in my mind that I'd rather not play than get so mercenary about it that I'd have to give up the things that made it fun.

This decision probably kept me from becoming a higher-ranked player sooner, but I didn't regret it at all and I still don't today. I've always put staying close to my friends and family as high on my list of priorities as I responsibly could. Some journalists have described me as a late bloomer, or a tortoise to the other guys' hares, but I never saw it that way. I've really just been going about my career in my own way, and part of that way is the acknowledgment that my life is about more than my tennis.

When I was laid up in that hospital room in Rome, I received a note from exactly one player from the tournament that was in town. *One.* Contrast that with all the friends who came to visit me daily, for months, when I was home sick with zoster, and you know why I feel as good as I do about my decision.

Beyond the perspective I was gaining on my friends' lives, I began to speculate about other people's lives. I would walk the streets in the daytime, running out to get some lunch or visit the bookstore, and during my strolls, I would realize that unless they were tennis fans, people who saw me, saw just another human being in their midst. They had no idea about the crossroads I was at in my life.

Looking at people as I passed them, I imagined their networks of friends and families—their coworkers and business associates who greeted them every day and cheered them up on Monday morning. I began watching people and wondering what they did for a living, and considering what they might be going through in their lives—a crisis as I was, or maybe some happy time, or perhaps just business as usual?

During these walks, I often found my mind drifting back to that morning in Newport when I learned of my father's death. I thought about how oblivious the people at breakfast had been to our pain, but also how oblivious I had been to their lives. Seated there on that morning, I had assumed that our table was the only one going through a tragedy when the reality was that that I had no idea what the state of the hearts and minds of those people were.

When you play tennis for a living, the world is pretty simple; it's the rest of the world and the rest of life that's much more complicated.

Toward the end of September, I got a great surprise from some other old friends. At the suggestion of the players, Davis Cup Captain Patrick McEnroe called and invited me to join the team, which included Mardy and Andy Roddick, during the preparation for its upcoming tie against Belarus in Charleston, South Carolina.

It was an amazing gesture. The Davis Cup was a source of some very important memories. Right after I left college, the USTA invited me to be a practice partner for the team in its tie against Australia in Chestnut Hill, Massachusetts, just outside Boston. The next thing I knew I was shaking hands with some of the best American players of the past decade, namely Pete Sampras, Jim Courier, and Todd Martin.

For a kid who had just turned pro, it was a thrill to get to know these guys—playing poker and going to baseball games in our downtime—and it was also a chance to glean some of their priceless wisdom. Pete Sampras gave me a piece of advice that I've kept to this day. "You have to have a short memory," he said, sharing what he saw as one of the secrets of championship play. "If you blow a point, or a game, or a set, just *forget it*." If you watched Sampras compete, then you know this was something he did all the time—his confidence was so steady that he could continue to hit aces and winners, often right after the most heartbreaking moments.

In 2001, I became a member of the Davis Cup team for the first time, winning my debut match, against Leander Paes of India. Playing on the team was always very special for me, not just for the honor of representing my country, but also because it gave me a chance to be out on the road competing *with* my friends instead of *against* them.

So when Patrick invited me to come down to Charleston, I jumped at the chance. I flew down and when I arrived at the practice courts, Patrick was hitting with Mardy. Pat left the court and Mardy and I began hitting with each other. It was just like old times: Mardy, who knows how much I hate being drop shot-ted, hit one my way, and I did what I always did: I took off sprint-ing across the court to track it down. I ran so fast that I actually slid on the hard court trying to get to the ball and pulled my groin muscle. The trainer evaluated my injury and told me not to hit anymore that week to avoid worsening it.

The rest of that week became the perfect metaphor for my life at the moment: I was on the bench, looking on as the tennis world went about its business without me. When the Bryan brothers won the doubles match, clinching victory for the United States, we all ran out on the court to celebrate, but when it came time to take the team picture, it was just the Bryans, Andy, and Mardy. I was thrilled for the guys, but I also felt farther away from the action than I ever had. It made me want to do whatever I could—doctor's orders be damned—to get it back, to get all of it back. This was where I wanted to be; now all I had to do was get better, so that I could be here.

———————

I came back from the Charleston trip fired up and ready to work. I met Brian at Fairfield University for our every-other-day practice and he instantly upped the ante with the ultimate lemonade-out-of-lemons game plan: "For the rest of the off-season," he told me, "we're only going to work on weaknesses."

It was a brilliant suggestion, and it couldn't have come at a better time. Like any player, I had things in my game that were liabilities, weaknesses that an astute opponent could pick on: my backhand wasn't a threat, and I was downright bad at controlling high-bouncing shots to that side. My slice backhand, a defensive shot that I had never really mastered, could use work, and I was pretty bad at hitting drop shots, and touch shots in general.

Rather than get frustrated by not being able to do things I was accustomed to doing well, Brian was saying that we should work on improving other things, the idea being that this up and down practice period could actually be a very well disguised gift—one capable of making this athletic isolation rewarding and ultimately helpful for my game. And so we started a new routine: we'd work about two hours each day, starting with thirty minutes of running drills to strengthen my lungs and my ability to stay on defense. After that, we'd work on drop shots and slice shots, over and over, and when we were through with those, I'd get behind the baseline and Brian would run me all over the place, while I simply tried to float balls back to his side of the net. We did this over and over and over—developing not only my defensive shots, but also my defensive *mind,* learning to be patient and bide my time until I drew an error from a frustrated opponent or got something to work with from him.

When the weather changed, Brian and I took our practices indoors at the Tennis Club of Trumbull, the same club at which we first met. All around me were reminders of my formative years of tennis. This was the place where I first began to understand my frustration on the court, and the positive energy of those lessons infused every session with Brian. Practicing alongside groups of other players, I came to see my good fortune for what it really was. On a few consecutive mornings, there were two guys taking a semiprivate lesson on the next court. I watched them out of the corner of my eye throughout their entire hour. They were older than I was, not in the best of shape, and the pro was helping them through the basics, periodically coming around to their side of the net to stand behind one of them and guide his hands through the motion of a proper forehand, or to demonstrate a serve. As I observed them on the court, I noticed that they were having a great time, and it struck me how incredibly lucky I'd been to find tennis as a child.

This in turn made me think about how cavalier I had been about my career my first few years on tour and how much harder I could have worked then. A lot of athletes have the attitude that they can improve next year, that they're doing well enough for now and they have all the time in the world. I was only twenty-four, but I was already dealing with the possibility that there might not be a next year. If it turned out that there would be another year, I decided that I'd work harder than I ever had before.

But still, as October turned into November, my up and down performance in practice continued. Working on the weak spots was helping, but the inconsistent nature of the practices made it hard to see the progress that was taking place. Part of the difficulty and the fun of Brian's getting-better approach was that I had to be able to see improvement in my performance and feel it within myself. But when every day seemed to pose a set of obstacles that was different from those of the previous day, it became much more difficult to discern whether improvement was actually taking place.

On November 16, I traveled to Atlanta to play an exhibition benefiting Robby Ginepri's Atlanta Youth Tennis Foundation. I knew I wasn't ready for a match, but I thought this would be a harmless place to get a little taste of the old action. Robby knew that I'd been sick, but I don't think he quite realized what I was dealing with. When we started playing, he was up on me in a hurry and I knew that if he turned it up I'd get crushed.

After the between-set changeover, when we passed each other at the net, I leaned in and whispered, as much for my own benefit as for the fans, "Let's make this close, or it might get embarrassing." He got the hint and we kept it interesting, but of course, in the end, I lost. It was just an exhibition but I took the loss like a real one because it made me wonder when and if I'd fully recover.

A few weeks later, on December 7, I played Mardy at a benefit in Vero Beach, Florida. I told him to play me for real, because January was coming, and with it the Hopman Cup, which I'd decided would mark my return to the tour, followed shortly by the Australian Open.

Mardy killed me in the first set, and on the changeover, I told him to keep it up. I needed the experience, even if the experience was losing, which it was.

After that event, I went back to Tampa and practiced harder than I had all fall. As was the case up North, I'd have a good day followed by a bad one, and vice versa. It was hard to be positive, but nothing was going to keep me from at least trying to compete again come January. I was done praying at the altar of patience; I was back to worshiping hard work.

A few days before Christmas, I headed home to Fairfield. The holidays were tough that year, especially for my mother. She only mentioned once how much she missed my father, and otherwise we didn't talk about him much, just trying to push on as he would have wanted. Three days later, for my birthday, about a dozen of us went out for dinner. We took it easy, since I didn't need or want a big blowout. I'd be leaving for Australia in the next forty-eight hours and wanted to keep myself in the best shape possible.

When I got home, I got ready for bed. I washed my face and, drying it off, caught a glimpse of myself in the mirror. Was it only a year ago that shaving my head was the biggest decision in my life?

I yawned. Although the left side of my face seemed to be functioning again, I noticed something that had continued, but which I hadn't told anyone else: my left eye still didn't open or close exactly the same way my right eye did. I guess that meant that the virus was still lingering, but I didn't care. I *had* to get back out on tour.

I got into bed and turned off the light. My house is only a few blocks away from the center of town, but by that hour it was already as silent outside as it was dark. I lay there and thought about the past several months. I didn't know what would happen when I got back out there in a few days, but I had realized that the lesson of 2004 was to treat my life as a sprint, not a marathon, to go after what I wanted even harder than before, and not to compromise.

So much had changed since I lay in the same bed twelve months ago—I'd lost my father, my ranking had plummeted to ninety-seven, and I had twice flirted with losing it all. And yet, the moment felt oddly familiar. Just a year earlier, I was lying in the same bed, envisioning the same blinding Australian sun pouring through the top of Rod Laver Arena. I pictured the court, and the thought alone seemed to welcome me and rejuvenate my spirit. I imagined the crowds, those thousands of faces that all blurred together when you looked up, and how, once in a while, you'd make direct eye contact with a little kid or some man or woman who you could just *feel* was pulling for you, even though you'd never met them and most likely never would.

I imagined the moment I had been waiting for all year, when the stadium MC would rattle off my list of career highlights and announce my name to the crowd and I'd look up from my warm-up and wave as they cheered. I didn't know how I'd do or where I'd end up, but I smiled myself right to sleep, happy just to have the opportunity again.

SIX

IF YOU CAN WIN ONE SET, YOU CAN WIN TWO

JANUARY–MAY 2005

As is our confidence, so is our capacity.

—WILLIAM HAZLITT

I showed up in Australia in January 2005 with a jumble of emotions in my heart—I could barely keep from grinning as I visualized the tournament grounds and what it would be like to reconnect with all the guys I hadn't seen since late summer, not to mention the tour itself, just to be around tennis, and the fans, and getting back to work. At the same time, I had no idea what to expect from the competition. My ambitions were a whole lot more modest than they had been a year earlier, when I was looking to take things to a new level. This was more of a scouting expedition—of *myself*—a return to play with the express and humbling purpose of seeing how it went. If Brian could have read my mind, he'd have been pleased because my only goal was, in the truest sense of the phrase, *getting better,* and learning if that was even possible.

I had been a professional player for four and a half years at that point, but after an absence of seven months, save for those few toe-in-the-water matches in the summer and fall, I felt like a rookie all over again. I was struck at the similarities between what lay before me and what awaited me right after I left college to go pro. Back then, I was taking an opportunity to see what I might pull off before time passed me by; now, I was taking an opportunity to see if my health had passed me by. A return to Harvard seemed as plausible in January 2005 as it did in June 1999, when I first tried my hand at this professional tennis thing.

My mindset was another matter. I had resolved not to put the same pressure on myself that I did in those earlier days. In part, this was thanks to all those courtside talks with Brian throughout the fall. Just like when I was a kid, his probing of what was going on between my ears had a direct impact on how I felt about what went on between the lines of the court. We hadn't just worked on weaknesses in my game; we had also worked on weaknesses in my thinking.

Looking back over my career, I had come to realize that

there was a big difference between working hard on my tennis and being hard on myself. The former was essential; the latter was self-destructive. I was open to this new point of view, in part, because where I used to feel I had to prove myself every time I went out on court, now I didn't feel the need to prove anything, at least not right out of the gate, to myself or to anybody else. Showing up was a victory in itself.

In many ways, I felt like a different person: Not only had the circumstances of my life changed—I still missed and thought about my father all the time—but this new attitude had me looking forward to competing in ways I hadn't been able to before, which let me relax, play my game, and enjoy the moment. I partnered with Megan Shaughnessy for the Hopman Cup and came out for my first singles match, against Peter Wessels of the Netherlands, like a bucking bronco. I was so excited to be back on court that I went for broke on every ball I had a good look at, and a majority of them landed right where I wanted them to. I was powered by an unprecedented adrenaline rush. Before I knew it, I had won. Wessels was ranked in the nineties at the time, but I felt like I'd just beaten the best player in the world.

I didn't win every match in the Hopman Cup, but I did well enough that the following week, when I traveled to Auckland to play in a tournament there, I felt good about my prospects. In some ways, Aukland would mark my true return to competition because it was the first event at which rankings points and prize money—the lifeblood of my sport—were at stake. My first-round opponent was Fernando Gonzalez, a Chilean who bears a striking resemblance to actor Benicio Del Toro. Fernando has one of the biggest forehands on the planet, and when I'm fit, watching us play is probably the closest it gets to watching two guys pummeling each other across a net. When I'm not fit, it's a different story. After losing a tight first set, I got blown away in the second, winning just one game.

Despite the disappointment, it was an instructive loss. We have a phrase in tennis: *match tough,* which I think of as confidence's cousin. It means that you've played a fair amount in the not-too-distant past and that your competitive instincts are honed. There's a rhythm to points in tennis, as well as a rhythm to games and matches, and even to tournaments, and this rhythm has nothing to do with how many hours you've logged on the practice court, or even how many exhibition matches you've played. When you're match tough you are accustomed to the big pressure moments and they don't faze you. Your emotional and physical stamina are ready for the rigors of a long contest, leaving you able to function on that plane of intuitive *acting* (rather than *thinking)* that inevitably produces your best tennis when you need it the most. You can *flow.*

Match tough also means that you've been out there contesting matches that *count,* that carry with them rankings points, prize money, and the prospect of either returning in a day or two for the next round or packing your bags, checking out, and getting on a plane. I had practiced my butt off in Fairfield and I had done well at the Hopman Cup, but my loss to Gonzalez showed me that I was still out of tune, still needed to knock the rust off my game and polish it up in order to compete in the big leagues again.

Being match tough builds up your immunity to the mysterious mind-body dynamics that can creep up on you during tournament play. Early in my career, I had a painful problem with leg cramping, usually in the late stages of a match. Some commentators unfairly knock cramping as a matter of conditioning only, when the truth is that you can cramp for all kinds of reasons—it can be triggered by stress or anxiety, or it can be caused by a deficiency of certain nutrients. I had worked for years to solve my cramping problems, but I had no idea if they might resurface the next time I found myself in the midst of a long, grueling match. Similarly I did not know if the emotion of the moment would overwhelm me and I'd suddenly find myself all used up, not cramping, but *spent,* with nothing left in the tank to allow me to think or move with authority. Simply put, I didn't have the confidence in my conditioning to know that I was match tough.

During the match with Gonzalez, I also became aware of a new dynamic in my point of view, something useful. Like many players, I was always apt to free-associate during a match, and as

I was about to serve, or sitting in my chair during the change-over, I'd remember similar moments from other matches, especially those against the guy I was playing. This could be useful, like if I recalled that a particular opponent had a tendency to lay off on his second serve or start pushing the ball at crunch time. But it could also be distracting if it forced me to remember some of my own pitfalls at a time when I should be thinking positively.

When I was playing Gonzalez, however, I wasn't thinking about past matches. I was calling on moments from the past few months. I'd think about how hard Brian and I had worked on all those weaknesses, all those hours I spent squeaking and sliding around behind the baseline floating balls back to him to improve my defense, or taking backhands down the line until they stopped going long or into the net and started landing right on the sideline, like an airplane touching down for a perfect landing in the center of the runway.

I also found myself thinking about my father—how much he had suffered and how quietly he had done it. While Brian's teaching over the years had greatly improved my on-court demeanor, all the teaching in the world couldn't have affected my court character the way the events of the past year had. During the Gonzalez match, I stayed positive and didn't get down on myself—not even in my head. The end result showed in my manner during the match. I was so gratified just to be on the court that I wasn't storming back to my chair on the changeovers after being broken, gritting my teeth and muttering to myself.

These thoughts of my father also impacted how I reacted to the match after I lost. I didn't take the loss the way I might have years earlier, staying up all night in my hotel room and nearly passing out to the sound of CNN or struggling to remain conscious through one more hand of online poker—doing *anything* to avoid being alone with my regrets of the day. If I felt myself getting negative, all I had to do was remember ten little words Dr. Kveton had said to me not six months earlier: *At least three months, or it could take four years.* I had come so close to losing it all and still didn't know if I could have it all back. That's what I was here to find out.

Not only that: After all those months wobbling around Fairfield, my first weeks in Australia were basically one long, drawn-out sigh of relief, because I was beginning to believe that, at the very least, I'd be able to keep playing *at some level* for the rest of my natural career.

Of course, I still had some doubts, but they were of a different variety. I was no longer envisioning the imaginary *SportsCenter* piece on my retirement, but I began to realize that staying optimistic on a day-to-day basis might be a little harder than I thought it would be. I began to focus on what was in front of me, and no matter how I sliced it, the loss was a loss. There were moments in the days after my match with Gonzalez when I thought about certain points and what I should have done differently to win them. I had made mistakes, some of which were frustrating, and despite my best efforts not to dwell on them, sometimes maintaining a positive approach was difficult.

By the time I got to Melbourne for the Australian Open, I had had time to reflect on all of this, and I began to think that I might not have had the right frame of mind when I had arrived in Auckland. Maybe getting better mentally would have to be like getting better physically—something that I'd have to approach one step at a time until I truly gave myself permission to just enjoy being out there and not put too much stock in any one win or loss.

When the day came to play my first-round match at the Australian Open, I had relaxed enough to go out and win 6–1, 6–2, 6–0, a huge moral victory because I had prided myself on not dropping a first-round match at a slam since my very first wildcard appearance at the US Open in 1999, when I was beaten badly on an outer court. I might have felt like a newbie all over again, but at least I wouldn't have to repeat that personal rite of passage. It was a relief.

Awaiting me in the second round was an opponent who brought back a lot of memories: Lleyton Hewitt. Lleyton had had a much better few years than I had since our fiery encounter at the US Open back in 2001. He had won two slams, finished 2001 and 2002 ranked number one in the world, and was coming into our match the number three player in the world to my number ninety-four. Not only that, but since this was the one hundredth anniversary of the Open, and with Pat Rafter retired, Lleyton was the great hope of the Aussies for their first native men's champion since 1976.

Lleyton and I hadn't become good friends since his outburst in 2001, but we had buried the hatchet—even practicing together a few times on the road. To me, this wasn't a grudge match; it was a huge opportunity.

Once again, I was having a burst of déjà vu, an emotional return to my first years on tour and a second-round slam match against Lleyton at a crossroads in my career. Once again, he was the heavy favorite. Once again, I had nothing to lose. The similarities were enough to give me goose bumps. By the afternoon of the match, my adrenaline level was so high that I *felt* totally healthy again, ready to get out there and run all day and kill the ball. One of the matches before mine went long, so I had to wait an eternity for ours to begin. I remember hanging out in the player's lounge for hours, my feet tapping incessantly because I could barely contain my excitement.

I had no idea what to expect but I almost didn't care. I was back where I loved to be, and I was about to have an honor granted to precious few players at any slam tournament—the opportunity to play on the center court, Rod Laver Arena in this case. Sure, they were putting us there because Lleyton was the number one player in his home country, but that didn't matter. I was about to experience all those things I loved, walking out onto the court with thousands of people looking on, hearing an announcer call out my name, and doing battle for a few hours.

By the time I was ushered out onto the court, it was so late that the lights had come on. The last match of the day-session was turning into a nighttime affair.

During the warm-up, I felt my excitement give way to a totally unexpected sense of calm. I was feeling the ball great and moving well. The gigantic overhead lights were illuminating the stadium like a movie set, and I had that good feeling of leaving my body a little bit, just enough to let the body take over, to operate on court sense and muscle memory and instinct and just flow.

That's exactly what I did: I came out on fire and took the first set 6–4. It went by in a flash, the way your best tennis always does. I was in a zone, almost delirious just from being out there and just letting it rip. It was like four years earlier at the US Open, except that the audience wasn't cheering for me. I was certainly the happiest person there, except maybe for Brian and my mom, who were in the box along with Mardy and Kevin O'Connor.

During the between-sets changeover (a slightly longer break than the one between games), I sat in my chair and did my best not to think about the fact that I had just taken a set off the number three player in the world a mere three weeks into my return, that I was up on a guy with whom I'd engaged in controversy a few years back under similar circumstances and lost. I tried not to think about the fact that television commentators, in a multitude of languages, were describing the potential upset playing out before them to viewers all over the world.

I tried not to think about any of that, because that's not how you win in tennis. Tennis is funny. No matter where in the world you are, the court is always seventy-eight feet long and twenty-seven feet wide (thirty-six if you're using the doubles alleys), and the net is thirty-six inches high at the center and forty-two inches high at the ends. Not only is the court the same, but if you're lucky enough to have a long career, the tennis gods will put you in the same *situation* more than once, maybe several times—it could be an opponent you've never beaten or who's come from behind to beat you, or a poor tiebreak record. Like most players, I had a few of those bugaboos in my portfolio: I'd never beaten Lleyton or Andy Roddick, I'd never been past the round of sixteen in a slam, I'd never cracked the top twenty, let alone the top ten, and I'd never won a five-set match.

It's one of those wonderful correlations between tennis and life: the only way to succeed where you've failed before is not to dwell on the past, but to keep your mind on the task before you.

One point at a time, I told myself, remembering my

hard-earned wisdom of the past several months. That's how you win at tennis, the same way you do in life, with patience and smarts, by keeping your wits about you.

It's a terrific challenge, because it's such a hard one: the only way to move on is to not focus on what you're moving on from.

One stroke at a time.

The chair umpire called "time," meaning it was time to get back on court and continue the match.

I managed to put it all out of my head in the second set and reaped the same rewards I had in the first: I got up a break and served for the set at 6–5. It was then that my lack of match toughness began to surface: not only were thoughts of the over-all match beginning to creep in, but I was beginning to think about the larger implications of winning this match, and doing it so soon after my return. I started to rush, even serving up a double-fault during the next game. I lost my serve, and we ended up at 6-games all, on the verge of a tie break.

Once again, I steadied the ship and earned a mini-break in the tie break, meaning I'd won a point on one of Lleyton's serve points. I was up 6–5. It was Lleyton's serve and he all but tapped a weak second serve to my backhand, but I hit it back tentatively and put it in the net. I cringed. All that hard work on my backhand in the fall and I was acting like my old self. But I did what Sampras had told me to all those years ago, and just put it behind me. I had been through too much to go back to my old habit of getting down on myself for one botched backhand.

A few moments later, Lleyton had a set point against me and again went to my backhand. This time I smacked it right down the line—a single stroke that uncorked months of pent-up frustration. It felt so good that I let out my own version of Lleyton's trademark scream: "Come on!"

But that was to be my last high point in the match. Too many mental pillars were beginning to collapse. I couldn't keep out all those thoughts and all that pressure, which made it nearly impossible to compete well in the big moments. Lleyton took that second set. By the third set, the lack of match play was taking its emotional and physical toll. I was exhausted and lost the set at love, which was especially sobering because I associated dropping sets at love with my 2003 slump. I wasn't getting down here the way I was then, but still it was dispiriting. I gathered myself together but it was too little, too late, and I lost the fourth set, and with it the match

I had lost, but I didn't even need time to reflect to see the positives; as I walked out of the stadium into the tunnel that lead to the locker room, waving up at the fans, I had the same feeling I'd had after that match I played with Lleyton in 2001. I felt like I had been born onto the tour all over again.

After the match, I had one of the longest, most personally revealing press conferences of my career. Because all of the major journalists come to the four slams, and because I had missed three of the slams a year earlier, there were reporters and columnists there I hadn't seen since the last Australian Open. They asked me as much about what I'd gone through back home as what I'd just experienced on the court, and they did so in a way that was surprisingly touching. It was a useful way to process the match out loud, and at one point, I put things in perspective, framing the loss in the context of what it had taken just to get there: "The worst thing that happened to me all day was I lost a tennis match."

———————

The flight home from any overseas tournament is a long one, but the flight back from Australia is the longest of all, more than twenty-four hours, including a stopover in Los Angeles.

That's a lot of time to be alone with your thoughts, and I spent much of those flights thinking about the Hewitt match and speculating about whether I could have won. When you're one point from a two-sets-to-none lead, you certainly have to believe that you could have done it, but I wasn't going to get down on myself for how things had turned out because there was too much to feel good about. It was like 2001 all over again, when Brian had walked with me in the hotel corridor afterward and told me that if I kept playing that way, I'd win plenty of matches. After my Job-like 2004, it was enough, for the moment, to know that.

Those first two sets had settled the matter of whether I could still play at a high level and it made me hungry for more and more match play, as well as more of that addictive crowd interaction. All I wanted to do was practice, get back out, compete, and fill my tank with as much match toughness and confidence as possible.

My next stop was Delray Beach, site of my last tour-level match in 2004. With all the enthusiasm I was carrying over from Australia, I couldn't have foreseen what would happen next. I came out for my first match, against Russian Teimuraz Gabashvili, a qualifier playing his first-ever match on a center court, and I felt totally flat from the first minute. It was exactly the opposite of the way I felt in Australia, but I couldn't put my finger on why. Whatever the reason, I didn't have any faith in my shots, and nothing was working. Somehow, I was able to eke out the first set, but then I just got outplayed for the last two.

I had no idea what to make of the loss. How was it possible to play Lleyton so tight in Australia and then turn around and lose so badly in Delray Beach? I thought of my dirty little secret—the fact that my eyes still didn't behave exactly the same—and wondered if maybe the zoster was still lingering. I remembered how throughout the previous fall, I'd have some of my best practice days ever, followed by days when I'd almost be tripping over my own legs, or struggling just to keep the ball inside the lines.

Dr. Kveton's words continued to echo. *At least three months, or it could take four years.* I felt certain that the virus was lingering, but was just as certain that there was nothing to do but press on and play through it. Coming back would require me to stay focused on the match before me, not on the big picture of my career. I needed to stay calm and take each day on its own terms.

Fortunately, I had friends to help me out, even though they weren't there with me. After Delray Beach, I sent out my results e-mail and when the responses started flying, I was sitting in my hotel room cracking up. As the reply e-mails came in, my laptop became my own portable version of my living room back in Fairfield.

I flew to San Jose, California, for another tournament the following week. At an off-site indoor tennis club where the organizers had arranged practice time for the players, I found the lighting a bit dim and was having trouble tracking the ball. I hollered over to Bobby Reynolds, a fellow American, on the next court.

"Does it feel dark to you in here?"

"Seems okay to me, James."

It was unclear what was going on—whether the lighting on my court was off or my vision was starting to betray me again.

I couldn't figure out what was wrong, but I didn't have time to debate it for long, and by the start of the tournament, my vision seemed good enough for me to play.

The tournament began promisingly when I beat South African Wes Moodie in the first round, but then I got crushed by Vince Spadea in two quick sets in the second. My match pattern that winter and spring was beginning to feel like my practice pattern back in the fall, a seemingly random progression of good days followed by bad days. I began talking to Brian openly about the very real possibility that the zoster wasn't totally eradicated, that perhaps it was more than just lack of match play. We didn't dwell on it, but despite all those positive signs in Australia, we were starting to wonder if I'd have to settle for something less than my old level again.

I was earning more frequent flyer miles than rankings points, but in spite of the letdowns, I was trying to keep my promise to myself to stay positive. This, however, began to get increasingly difficult when I flew back east, and Mardy Fish took me out in a third set tie break in the first round in Memphis, Tennessee.

In 2001, in Memphis, I had had one of the low points of my first few years on the tour, when I lost in the qualifying rounds to Scott Draper from Australia. Scott was a super-nice guy who was coming back not only from injury, but also from a devastating loss (his wife had died from cystic fibrosis). When he beat me in a third-set tie break, I was dejected and frustrated. I should have won, but didn't.

After that loss, I sat on the stoop outside the club that was hosting the tournament and called Todd Martin, who had become something of a mentor to me since I first met him during that Davis Cup weekend in 1999. I went into a manic rant about how I'd just lost a match I should have won, and how I didn't know why I was losing so much and that if I couldn't win more, then maybe I didn't belong on the tour, and that I couldn't take losing this much for the next twelve years, and on and on and on.

Todd talked me down off the ledge, telling me that everyone goes through this, that it's a rite of passage for a tennis player, that he believed in my ability, and on and on for about an hour.

In 2005, right back in that same town, playing the same tournament, I found myself experiencing the same sense of hopelessness. But this time I had my own experiences to draw on: I was going through the same evolution I had gone through four years earlier, when I was right out of college. In many ways the situation reminded me of another piece of advice that Todd once gave me about winning matches: if you win one set from an opponent you can win two. And if you win two, you can win three.

The same principle applied here: I had gone through the process of building up my confidence before, of honing my court sense and match toughness. That feeling I'd had on the flight to Australia at the beginning of the year—the feeling of being a rookie all over again—was more apt than I could possibly have known. Of course, I'd played professionally for five years, but when you stop what you're doing for as long as I had, you can't just leap back where you were. I kept thinking of those blisters that sprung up on my hands in the fall when I got back to work on the court—just as I'd lost my calluses on my hand, I'd lost them on my game.

Yes, I had done a lot of hard work on the practice court with Brian during the fall, and sure I had busted my butt in the gym during the off-season, but there was just no substitute for time on the tour.

I was receiving wildcards (direct entry into the main draw of a tournament, granted to a few select players at the discretion of the organizers) into a lot of events, but I couldn't string together more than two wins in a row. By the time the tour wound its way to the Masters event at Indian Wells, there were upticks in my game: I beat two quality players in the early rounds, Alberto Martin and current top ten player Nicolay Davydenko. That was a great week, because a bunch of the guys from back home, including Evan, Matt, J.P., Andy and his wife, Kristie, and even my original coach and owner of the Tennis Club of Trumbull, Ed Pagano, came out to join Brian for his fortieth birthday, surprising him at dinner just before my first-round match. A lot of them stayed around for my second-round match as well, and it was like old times to have them there cheering me on in the stands.

Nonetheless, I couldn't get past the third round. As much as the virus had affected me, I was beginning to realize that something else was going on: I felt like a bit of a pretender. Somehow despite all my rehab and all my practice, there was a part of me that didn't feel like I deserved to be out there with all these guys. My eight months off had changed everything, especially my sense of where I belonged.

You know what? I said to myself. *If I'm going to keep feeling like I did five years ago, I might as well go back and do what I did five years ago.*

I decided that I wanted to earn my way back, at least in my own mind, and to do it the same way I had as a rookie on the tour, by going back to the minor leagues and playing Challenger events. Not many players who have been in the top thirty voluntarily go back and play at that minor-league level, but it is an approach that had proven invaluable to some players in situations like mine, a way to rebuild their games and their confidence after coming back from protracted illness or injury. I was thankful that so many tournament directors saw fit to grant me wildcards, but I realized that I was ignoring some of my own newly minted wisdom. I wasn't *earning* the break I so desperately needed, I was relying on the good graces of others rather than proving it to myself.

This was a sobering realization. Before I came to this conclusion, I had been telling myself that I would be content to just be out on the tour, but the reality was that I was losing my right to even have that. By mid-April, I had lost early in another couple of events, and my ranking had slipped to 210, way outside what it would take to get into the main draw of tournaments.

I used to think that December was the time for me to step up and gaze into the abyss, to take stock of my tennis life. But I was peering into it eight months early when I made the decision to go back to the minor leagues and see how well I competed there. Maybe I could accept wildcards again in a little while, when I felt I deserved them, the same way I felt I deserved them back in 1999—because I would have given people a reason to believe they were well spent on me.

And, so, my next stop was Tunica, Mississippi.

Even tennis junkies probably don't know that there's a tournament in Tunica. The scene at a Challenger event is about as different from a tour-level event as you can get. There are no sponsor banners, no security, and no media.

The players at the Challenger level run the gamut from the up and coming to the down and out. There are new guys trolling for enough points to get directly into the main draw of the bigger events. There are young players trying to work out the kinks in their games; older guys trying to hang onto their careers by their fingernails; and career-Challenger players who either love tennis so much that they have made a decision to play at this level for as long as they can afford to, or guys who are so obsessed with the game that they are in a dysfunctional relationship with it and unable to move on. These Challenger tournaments have it all—optimism, pessimism, resentment, you name it.

What these events lack in glamour they more than make up for in intensity. It's a completely different dynamic at this level. If you're entrenched in the top fifty in the world, it's easy to have an "it's just a game" attitude about a loss, but here, your success really impacts your opponent: your points, money, and confidence come at the expense of his, and you both feel it a lot more than you would if you were playing on the main tour.

Like any Challenger event, the tournament itself operated on a different set of standards from tour-level events. Some Challenger tournaments lacked not only a sponsor-logoed scoreboard, but you actually had to turn your own scorecards on the changeovers. The crowd size would vary from event to event, but it was a far cry from the thousands of spectators who show up for tour-level action. The social aspect in Tunica was different as well: instead of running into the other players at the hot, local restaurant, we'd all see each other at Wendy's, which became the unofficial players lounge for the week.

There was always an element of danger to a Challenger event, because you never knew what to expect: Seasoned veterans didn't fear you at all, and they might even be hungrier than you are, quite literally because this is the place they come to put food on the table for their families. You can also be blindsided by a teenager you've never heard of who might be a future top five player and doling out the kind of fearless tennis that's unique to people who haven't turned twenty yet.

I felt like I was stepping up to the edge of that abyss almost every day. I won my first Tunica match pretty easily, but in the second round, I came up against Frenchman Jerome Golmard, then ranked number 263, who had been a top thirty player in his career and wasn't the least bit intimidated by me. I got down a break of serve in the third set, and suddenly, in the middle of nowhere, on a clay court, with ball kids standing in the wrong place and the spectators so close I could hear conversations, I was faced with the prospect of losing in the second round.

It was like being dropped through a trapdoor into my own past, right back to those days when I had no idea if I'd ever crack the top hundred, let alone the top fifty.

Golmard had been serving great the whole match, and I thought that if I could just get his returns in play that I would have a chance, but I just wasn't getting it done. Finally, though, I managed to break him back, and eventually I held on and won the match.

In the quarterfinals I played Paul Goldstein. Paul's one of the friendliest guys on the tour, a veteran who plays both tour-level and minor league events and has enjoyed his greatest success in his early thirties. I beat him, and he came to the net with a huge smile on his face, and gave me a big, firm handshake.

"Great to see you back, man," he said.

I thought about Paul, about how *grateful* he is to have the life he has, traveling the world and playing tennis for a living. He'd never made it quite as high in the rankings as I had, but he loved the life, and he kept getting better and better. I was struck at Paul's genuine happiness to see me back and doing well—the smile that broadened across his face as we shook hands at the net spoke volumes about not just his character, but also about what it meant to have the privilege to do what we do for a living—regardless of our ranking on a particular day. I took losses so hard that I don't think I'd ever been as happy for someone who'd beaten me as Paul was that day, but it gave me something else to think about.

It motivated me that I had inspired and earned that kind of respect, and that it had been communicated to me with such a simple gesture. I went on to win the semifinals and final without dropping a set.

Anyone reading about this in the papers at the time probably thought it was a head-scratcher—why was I playing Challengers when I was getting wildcards into tour-level

tournaments?—but it was my first title of any kind since win-ning in DC in 2002. I was the last guy standing at the end of the week, and for the first time in a year, I felt my reservoir of confi-dence was beginning to fill up again.

The next week, I traveled to Forest Hills, New York, and another clay-court Challenger, this one on the grounds of the former US Open site. I had a lot more fun there, because my mother came out to watch my matches, and Patrick McEnroe surprised me one day as well. Patrick was someone who under-stood what I was doing there: years earlier, on the strength of his family name, he'd been granted all kinds of wildcards when he was right out of college, but he decided to start qualifying for events rather than accepting their charity. It made him a better player, and a more confident one.

I got through my first three rounds at Forest Hills pretty easily, buoyed in part by some very welcome news. The Pilot Pen tournament, a women's tournament which for years had been played during the summer in New Haven, Connecticut (a short drive up the Merritt Parkway from my hometown of Fairfield), had just acquired a men's tournament to go along with the women's tournament. I was so excited that I had Carlos reach out to tournament director Anne Worcester, who used to be the CEO of the WTA, and get me into the draw.

By telephone, from the Forest Hills tournament, I joined Anne in a joint conference call with the media, in which the men's tournament was announced, and I was revealed as the first player to commit to playing there. I couldn't wait; my longtime dream of having a local tournament near Fairfield had come true. Finally, there would be an event to which I could invite my friends and family, that wouldn't require them to drive to New York City. All of a sudden, I felt like there was a little beacon of hope in my year, a lighthouse by which I could navigate the sea of uncertainty—there was now a homecoming to look forward to, and it was just twelve weeks away.

When the Forest Hills semifinals rolled around, my optimism was almost dampened by a near disaster. After winning the first set, I dropped the second in a tiebreaker, and in the third set, I found myself down two match points against an Argentine named Juan Pablo Brzezicki. There's such a fine line between having a full tank of confidence and seeing your needle drop down to empty all over again: if I had lost one of those points—if he had conjured up one go-for-broke winner or a lucky mishit that dropped in, all of my momentum of the past few weeks would have been stopped dead in its tracks.

How did this happen? I was just up 6–1 . . .

Focus. You've been here a million times before. C'mon focus.

I put the context out of my head. I concentrated on the next few points, and played them aggressively, but safely. I came back and won the third set, 7–5, then won the final, against Dusan Vemic (coincidentally the same guy Thomas had beaten in Newport the day my father passed away), and my mom, Caraly, Laura, Sara, and two other old friends, Brendan and Dan, were all there to see it. It was sweet. Even though all my wins were still in the minor leagues, there's nothing like ten victories (and two titles) in a row to make you feel good about your game, especially when you can share it with your friends and family—a little taste of what I was looking forward to in August at the Pilot Pen.

Unfortunately, there was no time to really celebrate because I had to get right to the airport for my flight to Paris. I thanked everybody for coming, took a quick shower, got in a car, and sped off to JFK. A year earlier, I had wanted to show that an American could succeed on the red dirt of European clay courts, now I just wanted to prove that I could still compete—there, or anywhere, at the tour level—and I wanted to do it the hard way: I have no idea if the French Tennis Federation would have granted me a wildcard in 2005, because I didn't ask for one. I decided to earn my way into that tournament by winning the three matches I'd need to qualify, to prove, one more time, that I still belonged out there.

SEVEN

FIRE IT UP ONE TIME . . . *BAM!*

MAY–AUGUST 2005

What is a friend? A single soul dwelling in two bodies.

—ARISTOTLE

My momentum made it across the Atlantic with me. I arrived in Paris on a redeye flight, but I wasn't about to let the rigors of travel slow me down. I cut through the qualifying rounds, winning another three matches on my least favorite surface, red clay, earning my way into the main draw of the French Open, then winning my first-round match, adding even more to my growing collection of consecutive wins.

The fits and starts that had begun the year had come to a halt; now my game was as consistent as my focus. The minor league tournaments were more helpful than I could have imagined. With so many wins under my belt, I was no longer merely probing the tour to see if I could eke out an existence there. Instead, I was coming into each match believing I could win, and once again, I was hungry for a whole new level of success. The victories put me back in touch with that burning desire for advancement that had been dormant for so long.

Not only were the fits and starts of my game being smoothed out, but so were the fits and starts in my playing life. Owing to my neck injury in 2004, I hadn't played in a Grand Slam tournament other than the Australian Open in *two* years, so moving into the clay-court season and knowing I'd continue on toward the grass-court season and Wimbledon was tremendously reassuring.

I exited that French Open following a tough five-set encounter in the second round, but I didn't let it get me down. Just the opposite, in fact. The simple truth was that I hadn't played so much tennis in such a short time in over a year and there were no two ways about it. Not only was my body getting acclimated to life on the tour, it was getting used to *winning* again—because the more you win, the more you play. It was a nice problem to have. My legs were fatigued, my shoulder was sore, and my back ached, but the reason behind it all was good news that trumped any discomfort I might be feeling.

I was also, finally, starting to feel like my old self again, like a seasoned professional player accustomed to the rhythm of the life. You get used to a lot of international travel in my line of work, and at some point you just kind of go numb to it. You become adept at catching sleep where and when you need it—taxicabs, airport lounges, wherever—and develop the ability to shut out the jetlag when it's time to get on court and compete.

Though I felt right at home getting back into the traveling life, my overseas travel was affecting me in new ways. I came to think of it as *life*lag, the feeling that I was a man out of time, constantly flitting back and forth between the present and the past. In much the same way that playing tennis offers you the opportunity to repeat moments, just being on the road and *around* tennis was causing me to relive some of the most important events in my life. The red clay in Europe brought back the day in Rome when I had fractured my neck, and every time I set foot on the powdery dirt of a court, I'd steal a glance at the net post. Staring at the unforgiving shine of the metal, I could hear Dr. Lutz's words echoing in my ears, telling me if I hadn't turned my head before impact, I'd have likely been paralyzed.

Moving seamlessly between past and present, I remembered anew how lucky I was just to be able to stand up—let alone play tennis, let alone play it for a living. As I examined my surroundings, I thought of how many times I'd been to Paris and other cities around the world before 2004 and never really stopped to soak them in—even if, due to my tight schedule, that meant simply appreciating them a little more while I zipped around in the car.

A few weeks later, I returned to Wimbledon for the first time since 2003.

Having made it to the third round of a warm-up event prior to Wimbledon, I was still pretty depleted, and so I bowed out in the first round there. I tried my hardest, but there wasn't a whole lot I could do about it; my opponent played well and my body was beginning to protest as I cramped in the fourth and final set.

It was the first time since my freshman year on tour that I had lost in the opening round of a major, but the site of the loss kept things in perspective: the Old England Lawn Tennis and Croquet Club, which hosts the Championships, is a grassy, hilly retreat on the outskirts of London—in many ways it feels like a college campus with courts in place of classrooms, and it's the perfect setting for reflection. I was exhausted, but it was the price of success in those Challenger events, the cost of qualifying for the French Open, the cost of earning my way back to where I wanted to be.

A few years earlier, my loss at Wimbledon would have had a devastating impact on my confidence, and I would have taken it as a sure sign that I was failing in my mission. But that's not what happened to me after the match. On the contrary I found myself feeling buoyed by the effort I had displayed not just at

Wimbledon but in all of my European matches. After Wimbledon, I knew deep inside that I was on the right track, that I was pushing my body and soul to the maximum and leaving everything I had on the court. As my father might have said, you can't ask any more of somebody than that.

Walking the grounds after that match, my lifelag was all around me, as I thought of that day, two years prior, when my mother pulled Thomas and me aside and told us how my father had gone incommunicado. My stomach tightened as I revisited the details from that day—tracking her down at home in the middle of the night, hearing word of my dad's dire condition, and waiting on the excruciatingly long flight home to be with them. Going even farther back, I found myself sitting with my brother, as my father told us that we would never be able to control our level of talent, only our level of effort, and counseled us never to stop believing in the power of hard work.

I stopped on one of the club's lush hills and paused for a moment, catching a momentary glimpse of my courtside chats with Brian when I was a little kid. I reentered the anger and frustration of my past and redrew the connections between my behavior on the court and my life outside the lines.

Sewing everything together, I came to see that the shape of my personal life and this complex web of history and advice were the things that had allowed my career to continue in spite of everything that I had been through. I wondered where I would have been if it hadn't been for these two mentors. If not for all the wisdom they imparted on me when I was younger, I never would have had the patience to repeat all the rites of passage I'd had over the past few months. The events of 2004 were the realization of everything that I had been raised on, and without them, I would not have been standing on the green landscape of Wimbledon, England.

As things started to click again, I realized that the challenges of 2004 were fueling my drive in 2005 and giving me the ability to persevere and recognize that if I took it one day, one match, one step at a time—on the court and off—I would prevail. Since getting back on tour in January 2005, I had been so devoted to rebuilding my game that I still wasn't fully appreciating what I'd gone through the previous summer and fall. Now that my game was showing signs of life, I let myself reminisce about my time at home in 2004—all those lunchtime visits with my father, all those hospital stays, mourning his death, and then my own sickness and the long, long months it took to recover from it all—medically, physically, and emotionally.

Like the French Open, I didn't make it as far in Wimbledon that year as I would have liked, but where as a disappointing performance might have derailed my resolve in years past, this time was different. My exit represented a meager withdrawal from the account of confidence and momentum that I had amassed with my consecutive wins in the spring, and I didn't need a scoreboard to let me know how I was doing: I *knew* that I was back on the right track, and that I was living up to my lifetime goal of getting better that had never been more relevant or useful.

I was so sure that I had a big summer in store for me that I couldn't wait to get back to the United States. I love the challenge of playing on clay and grass, but with my swelling anticipation I was eager to get back to the hard courts of my home country, the surface on which I was raised and had always had my best results. For the first time in three years, I was coming back to something positive: in 2003, I had rushed home from England to be with my ailing father. In 2004, I had come home to rehab my neck. But now, I was flying west across the Atlantic with my thoughts focused firmly on the North Star of my year, the Pilot Pen tournament in New Haven, that home-state event to which I had committed back in May. I was absolutely determined to maintain my momentum until I got there, to really bring it home, literally and figuratively, and make something special happen right there in my friends' and my collective backyard.

In early August, just a few weeks before the Pilot Pen, I returned to the Legg Mason Classic in Washington, DC, the site of both the highest and lowest points of my career—my lone ATP title in 2002 and my embarrassing never-should-have-done-it appearance in 2004. Once again, tennis had thrown me the chance to relive, and maybe rewrite, my past.

Evan came down from Fairfield to be with me in DC. Having a friend from home in the box with Brian has always been a good omen for me, and my first match gave me more cause for celebration than anything in months, a straightforward, straight-sets victory. In the next two rounds, I was challenged in three-set encounters, but I held on and won both, including a second-round win over eighteenth-ranked Radek Stepanek, another huge boost, since I was ranked just outside the top one hundred at the time.

The week flew by, one win followed by another, and before long I felt like I was living 2002 all over again; if the zoster was still lingering, I sure wasn't feeling it. Instead I had that air of invincibility that clicks in at a certain point during an "up" period in your playing life. J. P. Johnson, one of the gang from Fairfield, came down toward the end of the week to join Evan, and I had to wonder, again, if it was mere coincidence that I seemed to play my best when my friends were there cheering me on.

Come the weekend, I was positively soaring. I made it to the final, my first Sunday showing in a tour-level event since 2003. I didn't win—Andy Roddick took me out, extending his winning streak over me to six in a row—but it was still an awesome and encouraging week. Of course, hoisting the trophy would have been the perfect ending, but in some ways, it was the ideal prelude to New Haven. In this year of rebirth, I had redone almost everything I had done earlier in my career: I had played in a few major tournaments, I had gone back to the minor leagues and won two tournaments there, and now I had made it to a final in a tour-level event.

All that was left was to actually score a title, and there was no better place for my comeback to peak than the first-ever Pilot Pen men's tournament in Connecticut.

To head there for something I was actually looking forward to was almost enough to bring tears to my eyes. It felt a bit odd, almost eerie, to arrive in the doorway of my own house, in my hometown, my tennis gear slung over one shoulder, my duffel bag over another, like a guy returning home from a business trip, but at the same time, it felt good to be home.

Just walking into the living room brought back all those evenings passed there with Evan, Matt, J.P., and the rest of my friends the prior fall, playing poker, or dispatching someone on a chicken wings and burger run to Archie Moore's, the local pub that served as our unofficial canteen. I remembered all those people I hadn't seen or heard from in years—friends from high school, and friends of friends, and the parents of friends—who had dropped in to see me, bringing me a card or a home-cooked meal. I remembered my parents coming over for my father's last Christmas with us in 2003 and how he beamed when he gave me the bracelet that I still wear to this day.

My ranking was in the low sixties that week, still well below what it had been when I got hurt, low enough that I needed a wildcard to get into the Pilot Pen, but I couldn't have cared less. It felt so good to have a real home to return to, the place that I came to when my neck was fractured, or when my body was ravaged by that virus. Nothing could compete with the satisfaction of knowing that there was an entire community out there that cared about me and would've cared about me whether or not I ever played another professional match. I had known this for years, of course, but standing there in my living room with my tennis gear in hand, I felt it wash over me like something realized for the first time.

It was my turn now. After all those hours everyone spent looking after me in 2004, keeping me company at home, or dragging me out the door, frozen face and all, for a night on the town, it was my turn to do something for them. It was my turn to do something for my mother, who had been through so much over the past few years, and had been there for me less than a week after burying my father. It was also my turn to do something for Dad, to turn in a performance that would have made him proud in the community where he and Mom had raised us.

Back on that conference call from Forest Hills, I had put tournament director Anne Worcester, whom I had never met, on the spot in a very public way: "I'm going to need a lot of tickets," I told her. "I have a ton of friends in the area and we've all been through a lot together. This would be something really special for them, to come see me play."

Once we were off the media call, and had a chance to speak privately, Anne got back to me on my request: "No problem," she said. "We'll put aside fifty seats and set up a special area for them."

I cringed. My parents didn't raise me to be greedy, but I needed more: "I *really* appreciate that, Anne, but I might actually need more than that. I'm happy to pay for them."

"Don't worry, James," she said. "We'll work it out."

I just wanted the seats so that my friends could hang out together and enjoy a night of tennis for as long as I stayed in the tournament. But Anne was eager to promote her new men's tournament, and thought it would be media-worthy to actually name the private cheering section of the hometown player.

"What do you think?" she said. "How about maybe Blake's Backers? Or Blake's Bunch? Something to let everyone know that these are your fans?"

I thought it was a cool idea, and I suggested using my initials in the name. She put the question to her marketing team, and they hit on the name that she thought would work best: The J-Block. I loved it. Not only because it made an indelible impression, but also because it perfectly summed up what my friends were to me—they were my block, my rock, the people who got me through my troubles in 2004, and the people who would be there for me in future years.

She was getting excited: "Maybe we should get them megaphones, or something, so they can really make some noise."

"You know something, Anne," I said, remembering how much noise just a handful of my friends were capable of making when they came to see me on the road, or at the US Open. "I think they'll be loud enough on their own."

———

"James! James! James"

I could hear the chanting as soon as I walked out onto center court for my opening round match, against Michael Llodra from France, then ranked number sixty-nine in the world.

"James! James! James!"

In the special seating area behind the baseline on the north side of the court were all my friends, all those men and women who had seen me through 2004. They were on their feet, shaking their fists in the air, and chanting my name, rhythmically, like a war cry: "James! James! James!"

I couldn't believe how many of them had shown up. Some of them had traveled on occasion to watch me on the road, or even overseas. But on this night, *all* of my close friends from Fairfield were there—the ones I went to junior high with, the ones I played junior tennis with, the ones who moved there after college. The only place where I had ever seen them all gathered in one place before was my father's funeral a little more than a year earlier. There had to be at least fifty of them and they were all fired up and shouting right to me.

They were also in *uniform:* Brian's pal Bobby D. had twenty-five T-shirts made up for the occasion. They were Carolina blue (my favorite color) with the phrase "Fire it up one time . . . *Bam!*" emblazoned on them. It was an in-joke. Years earlier, Brian's friend Andy Jorgensen, a big muscle-bound guy with unmistakable locks of golden-blond hair, was at a boring party and began muttering to himself, "C'mon, people. Fire it up one time. *Bam! Bam!*" He would do this at every such party. Most people never noticed him doing this, but Brian and I always did, and we both thought it was hysterical. In time, it became a phrase used by our inner circle, something we'd say when someone won a big pot in poker, or hit a great shot in tennis.

And, if that weren't enough, there was also a J-Block banner draped behind them.

Thanks to the matching shirts and the way the banner framed them, my friends didn't look like just a random bunch of tennis fans: they looked like something more, like a choir—a screaming, chanting, beer-swilling, high-fiving choir.

I put on a show for my friends that night: I won the match in two quick sets and the whole time, the J-Block was cheering for every winner I hit as though their lives depended on it.

I've always been proud that my player's box is usually full at tournaments, even in faraway places. I've got enough friends on the tour, and around the country, that there are always people I want to have there alongside Brian. But every time I looked up at the J-Block that night, I realized that these people were always in my player's box as well, even though they were rarely there in person. Every one of those J-Blockers was there with me on the road, watching over me just as surely as they were there looking down on me from the stands on that August evening in New Haven.

As much as I appreciated everything they had done for me when I was sick, once I had returned to the tour, I had gotten right back into my old frame of mind, focusing on nothing but the next match or the next practice, or the next interview or promotional event. It's hard to avoid this mindset because life on the road just never stops, and as such, I didn't always stop to think about whether my friends were supporting me when I wasn't there. Oh, sure, I knew that they followed my matches. Whenever I sent out my results e-mail, then started receiving replies, I was always surprised at how many of them always seemed to know the score already, either from watching on television or by following the match on the Internet, sitting for hours as point after point registered on a virtual scoreboard. But now, with my friends *literally* there looking over me, I remembered all over again how much I owed each of them, because if it weren't for them, I never would have gotten back out there.

I also felt my father with me, looking down from high above the stadium. I still thought about him all the time while playing matches, but standing there on the court in New Haven, I felt him more powerfully than ever, with everyone whose lives he had touched watching me play and seeing that my perseverance was testament to his legacy. He might not have been there during my zoster days, but he got me through them as much as those friends who visited me all the time. The memory of him was reflected in their faces and posters—the signs that dangled from the rafters above their heads.

I had never been more thankful for the decisions my parents made for me as a child than I was that night. What if I'd shipped out to a tennis academy as a little kid or stopped playing for my high school team because I was "too good?" What if I'd been denied the normal childhood I cherished so much, the childhood that resulted in the rows of people standing in front of me? Maybe I would've won more tournaments by the time I was twenty, but who would have been there for me in 2004, when I needed friends who would just show up? If not for the priorities my parents had chosen for me before I was old enough to choose them for myself, I surely wouldn't have had all these friends, not even a fraction of them. Maybe none of them.

Afterward, asked by reporters about my cheering section, Anne explained that I was from the area, that these were my friends, that they would be there for all of my matches, and that they were called the J-Block. The name stuck. It was mentioned in just about every newspaper and wire story that covered the match.

When I won my first-round match, people who knew me began to come out of the woodwork, not just my old friends, but also Thomas's friends, and Brian's friends, and parents of friends, and people who took lessons from my friends at the local club and on and on. The whole phenomenon paralleled what had transpired almost exactly a year before: just as people I hadn't seen in ages had flocked to my door to wish me well when they heard I was sick, now they were showing up to share the moment with me when I was doing well. It was an unbelievable display of support; the supposedly "normal" part of my life was beginning to seem as extraordinary and dreamlike as anything I'd ever experienced on the pro tennis tour.

Also touching was the fact that tournament-goers began requesting seats adjacent to the J-Block so that they could join my supporters. This was more than all right with me—I was flattered that so many strangers were taking an interest in my story. The ever-expanding size of the J-Block earned it even more press attention, and before long every tennis fan in America had heard 'bout these incredible friends of mine, and our little extended family in Fairfield, Trumbull, and a handful of other towns clustered together there in our little county of Connecticut.

But there were a lot of people who don't know about the J-Block.

First of all, there's the rules. The J-Block can be pretty animated between points, games, and sets, but they also observe basic tennis etiquette: they don't applaud my opponent's errors, they are *silent* during the points themselves, they don't scream into their cell phones, and they keep it clean. This was largely thanks to Bobby D., who gave a little pre-game talk to the Block before each match, going over the dos and don'ts. If a newcomer to the group did something inappropriate during a match, like calling something out during a point, Bobby would be dispatched to administer a friendly crash course in Block etiquette.

The other thing people don't realize about the J-Block is that it comes with its very own managing director, namely Evan. When Evan graduated from college in 2002, his father's present to him was sending him on the road with me from the French Open through the US Open. Because he had gotten to know other players and learned how to operate behind the scenes a little, Evan was the guy who would secure seats for my friends, working with me to determine who sat in the player's box for each match, while begging for and borrowing tickets from the tournament and other players as we needed them.

Even after 2002, Evan would periodically come out on the

road with me for a tournament, taking time off from the club where he taught, and from helping his father with his real estate business, to spend a week with me and Brian. On these trips, he appointed himself "special assistant," coordinating the box seats, making dinner reservations, even running errands like picking up some Gatorade if we ran out. I never asked Evan to manage the J-Block for me; he assumed the role naturally and without asking anything in return, another instance of my having the right friends, because I'd never think to saddle one of them with such a task.

Running the J-Block was a monumental undertaking from Day One, and it snowballed in scale every day of the New Haven tournament; not only did he determine who was sitting where in the Block, but as the week wore on, he had to constantly visit Anne's office to request additional tickets, then scurry around the grounds of the tournament, or call around to dozens of cell phones, to track down friends and distribute them. Evan, who always sat with Brian in the player's box, also helped Bobby D. keep the group under control, texting Bobby if he noticed something inappropriate from his unique vantage point.

Just as all this J-Block momentum was really starting to build, I came out to play my third-round match against Tommy Haas, a German player who was trained at Nick Bollettieri's famous academy in Florida. Tommy had suffered through some injuries in recent years, but he was once ranked as high as number two in the world. A very complete player without an obvious weakness to attack, he's the kind of guy nobody likes to see looming in their half of the draw.

I came out that night and, though they started off as rowdy as ever, the J-Block was single-handedly silenced by Tommy, who was firing on all cylinders and crushed me 6–1 in the first set. I wasn't doing a thing wrong. I just happened to be up against a guy who was on fire, seeing the ball big, and exploding with confidence. If I put a first serve in, he'd rip it past me. A second serve? Forget about it. I'd think I had him on the ropes in a point, and he'd hit a miracle winner. I looked over at Brian and he just shrugged: sometimes the other guy is zoning, operating on a level beyond thought and strategy, and there's nothing you can do about it except ride it out and stay positive and hope he can't keep it up for two sets.

After the set, I dropped down in my chair for the change-over, the brief break before the next set began, still stunned and smarting from the beating I'd just endured. It's moments like these that make tennis a singular sport, because unlike boxing where you have your trainer and corner team to pump you up, or football when you have the sanctuary of the huddle, or just about any other sport you can think of, in tennis you are on your own for the duration of the match. Nobody can solve your problem but you. I thought of my father as I was sitting there contemplating the next set, of his admonishing me when I was little and instructing me: "If you have a problem, you *fix* it." He may have been more concerned with academics than tennis, but this particular philosophy of his couldn't have been more well suited to my sport and my current situation.

I looked up at all my friends up in their section, on their feet. During the opening set, I hadn't really focused on them because I needed to concentrate on what was happening on the court, but now I couldn't help but notice them. They were all screaming right at me: "C'mon, James!" "You can do it, James!" I'm sure that their T-shirts made them seem interchangeable to the people who read about them or saw them on television, but each one meant something specific to me: seeing Laura there I remembered how much she had helped me that day I came home from the hospital, coming to grips for the first time with the reality of my father's failing health. Seeing Matt, with his camouflage baseball cap turned backward, I remembered all our years together playing doubles in the juniors, crashing at his family's house when we were in Massachusetts, or the way he came into the hospital room when I was first diagnosed with zoster and cracked me up by telling me I looked ridiculous. I saw Andy there and remembered how his offhand muttering at parties had inspired the shirts they were all wearing, or Bobby and his generosity in having the shirts made. I saw Caraly and remembered how she had helped me trim my hair the night I decided to go bald and how excited she was for me and the coming year in 2004, before all those crises struck.

They came to form a single being, an individual who was standing over me, saying that I could do it, that my hard work was for a reason. I saw all of them together, and for the first time in over year, I saw my father.

Once again, I couldn't help thinking how the moment mirrored the previous year, when they were cheering me on through my long battle with zoster. Only this time, I didn't need to wait patiently for something beyond my control to pass; I could impose myself on the situation. Two years earlier I would have been down and out after a set like that, but getting down and out just wasn't an option that night. All of those people had poured so much of themselves into getting me back on that court that I simply had to turn it around, to come up with something special that we could all share, something to really mark how far we'd all come together.

When the umpire called "time," I got up and dug in. I played some points patiently, waiting for the right moment to go for a winner, and I played other points with abandon, going for a little more than I normally would just to keep the ball away from his hot hand. It worked: I won the second set, and every point I took was punctuated by a huge, collective scream from the J-Block.

Now Tommy and I were in a dogfight, only I was coming out on top. We played a number of intense, physical points, but I was scrambling so effectively that I was prevailing in the majority of them. No matter what he did, it seemed like I was getting to all the balls he put in my side of the court and getting them past him when I had to. I felt that desirable sensation of leaving my body, of moving up to that plane of peak performance, of flow, of operating on pure instinct and desire. My entire being was devoted to nothing but getting that little yellow-green ball off my side of the court and past the player across the net from me. There was no thought attached to my actions, it was all just happening, so much so that at some point I began to feel that I wasn't on the court at all, that I was up there with the J-Block, amidst my friends, *ooohing* and *ahhing* right along with them, or even above them, with my father, watching the performance, and nodding our approval in unison.

Next thing I knew, I had won the match, and I was back on the court looking up at my friends again as they went positively nuts celebrating the comeback. I was as confident as ever, but the win didn't have much to do with it. I had a new lease on life. I had had to work so hard just to be able to be out there, and now I had a fresh appreciation for it all. I felt like I was finally living all the changes I was hoping to implement back in January 2004. In my next two matches, I won the first set and dropped the second, but I didn't get down the way I might have a few years earlier. I just stayed with it and won them both in three sets, and for the second time that month, I was in a final.

I could hardly believe it. Before 2005, I'd only been in four finals in my entire *career;* now on the heels of all that adversity, I was in my second final in four weeks. My opponent there was Spaniard Feliciano Lopez, a big-serving lefty who had just made it to the quarterfinals of Wimbledon earlier that summer. I got off to a bad start: Lopez won eleven of the set's last twelve points, taking it in just twenty-four minutes.

Then, in the second set, it started raining.

There's a loophole in the ATP's no-coaching rule: if there's a rain delay, you can get all the coaching you want, and in the locker room, I consulted with Brian. We agreed on a few simple adjustments, one of which was for me to just play my game and not be so hesitant. I think the prospect of winning my first tour-level title in three years was getting to me, and that was really all I needed to hear. I came back and won the next two sets, and the match, and with the J-Block hanging on my every shot. They felt the pressure right along with me and they celebrated the wins along with me. Not only were they chanting "James, James, James," but they'd huddle and come up with unified chants for certain occasions in the match; for example, if I had lost my serve, they'd start cheering "Break Time" during the next game, encouraging me to break right back.

It was my first tour-level title since 2002, but there was

almost no time to enjoy the moment. The tournament staff let all my friends—by this point we had secured tickets for more than one hundred twenty people—into the players lounge for a quick celebration, then I drove home to my house in Fairfield, where a car and driver we'd arranged ahead of time were waiting. He took me to my hotel in New York City, where the US Open was set to start the very next day. I checked in, ran around the corner to get a sandwich from a deli, came back to my room, and went to bed.

————

Talk about momentum: when I took on my first-round opponent in the US Open, Greg Rusedski, a former finalist there, I felt like I'd been shot out of a cannon and right through whoever was standing in my way. I beat him in straight sets, and then took out Russian Igor Andreev in the same fashion in the second round. An overwhelming number of my J-Block friends kept the party going, coming all the way down to New York to watch my matches, which was no small feat for most of them, because it required their using up vacation days or personal days at work or staggering into their jobs the day following a night match after trekking all the way back up to Connecticut, where most of them lived.

The J-Block was also taking on a life of its own. In the space of just one week, Nike had begun producing J-Block

T-shirts with an improvised J-Block logo on the front, and "F_
It Up One Time . . . *Bam!*" on the back. Not only did they provide these shirts to the J-Block itself, but they also sold them at
their kiosks on the tournament grounds. Because of what the
J-Block represented to me, I wanted there to be a charity com-
ponent to their sale, and so Nike agreed to donate all of the proceeds to Memorial Sloan-Kettering Cancer Center, where my
dad had been treated when he was sick. It was an incredible gesture on their part, and once again made me thankful for all I had
put into the relationships in my life, because that investment was
paying off big time.

I entered the third round as much of an underdog as I
had been in any match since my first years on tour. My opponent
was Spaniard Rafael Nadal, and we met on Ashe Stadium on
an absolutely perfect Saturday afternoon of Labor Day weekend. Nadal wasn't the number one player in the world, but he
was the number two, and he was the hottest thing going. He
had just won the French Open, and had shattered any notions
that he was a clay-court specialist when he beat Andre Agassi in
the finals of Montreal, a hard-court event, just a few weeks
prior.

I'd never played Nadal, but there seemed to be plenty to
fear: At just nineteen years of age, he was supremely confident
and had a very imposing presence and a feverish intensity. Not
only could he run down shots that most guys could only admire,

t he was also already known for leaping around after big points like he had just won the lottery.

It was an intimidating roadblock, but it did little to faze me. For all of the patience I had nurtured over the past year, the truth was that, in my heart, I liked to play high-risk, go-for-broke tennis, and Nadal was a guy against whom that actually made sense. I came into the match with the only game plan imaginable: to blast my forehand whenever possible and get into the net whenever I had the chance and end points. I didn't care that we had worked on my defense so much a year earlier, this wasn't the time to use it because nobody, and I mean *nobody*, was going to out defense Nadal. The only thing to do was keep the heat on.

That's how I played, with the J-Block urging me on at every step of the way. There were more than twenty thousand fans there that day, but at times I felt like my friends were the only ones watching me, along with Brian, Thomas, Evan, and my mother in the player's box. During some moments, the place was rocked with deafening cheers, but I could swear that the only sound I heard was that chant that seemed to be echoing down from New Haven . . . "James! James! James!" . . . that chant that had become like an internal soundtrack to my summer. The words urged me on point by point until I won the first set.

The J-Block's euphoria was dampened when Nadal took the second set. This was the danger point: the moment when self-doubt used to creep in, especially on such a big occasion. No disrespect to those guys I played in New Haven, but it's one thing to be down a set there and another to be one set apiece with the number two player in the world on Arthur Ashe Stadium. I thought about Todd Martin's old advice, that if you can win one set against an opponent, you can win two, and if you win two you can win three. I *had* just won a set a few minutes ago, so *of course* I could come back and win two more.

And, much as I had during that match against Haas in Connecticut, I thought about all my friends. After what it took for all of us to get there, what was a set? What was a point? What did I have to fear between the lines of a tennis court?

In my head I decided that it was clean-slate time: this was now a two-out-of-three-set match that I could win. I stayed patient, and with my friends trumpeting every point I won, I took the third set, finishing it off in style with two unforgettable flourishes—one of the best topspin lobs I'd ever hit in my life, followed by an emphatic overhead smash that ended the set with an exclamation point.

Two sets to one.

In the fourth set, the entire stadium felt like one giant J-Block. This was, after all, my country's Grand Slam tournament and so many Americans had followed my story in the news over the past year. When I looked up into the stands, my eyes would lock on those Carolina blue J-Block T-shirts scattered about, and I'd notice people pulling for me in ways I never had before. Many of them seemed as invested in my success or failure as my own friends and family were, raising clenched fists in my direction after I hit a great shot or leaning forward on their feet and just screaming encouragement at me.

The fourth set went by in a flash. Toward the end, mistakes started to flow from Nadal's racket in a way that I never could have imagined. With a little help from the people in the stands, my plan had worked better than I ever knew it could.

On match point, I came to net behind a pretty lame forehand approach shot that I felt sure he'd whip by me. I got ready to guess which way he was going to go . . .

. . . and he put the ball right in the middle of the net.

It was over.

I had won.

All of Ashe Stadium was on its feet giving me an ovation the likes of which I'd never heard before. From the court I had come to a year earlier to participate in Kids Day for maybe the last time, I looked up at the crowd and smiled at them. I was so overjoyed that I didn't even know how to express it. I squatted down right there on the court, looked up at my box, and then at the J-Block, and just shook my head. Who could've imagined we'd all be at a moment like this twelve months earlier, when we were all visiting in my living room up in Fairfield and I could barely get up off the couch without wobbling?

For the first time in my career, I was into the fourth round of my home country's Grand Slam event, the US Open, among the last sixteen men in the draw.

I had just hit the snooze button: the dream could go on.

———

Chair umpire Carlos Bernardes spoke into his microphone: "Game Blake. Six games all. Final set tie break."

I didn't need to hear the words. I knew the score. And it was a good thing, too, because I sure couldn't hear him across the short distance from his chair to the baseline, and I could barely make him out over the sound system. The noise from the crowd—twenty-some *thousand* people sending up a thunderous crescendo—caused the cement beneath my feet to quake.

It was almost one in the morning in early September 2005, and I was standing in the well of Arthur Ashe Stadium, playing in the quarterfinals of the US Open, my first-ever quarterfinal showing in a slam, having beaten Spaniard Tommy Robredo in the fourth round, following that victory over Nadal. Standing on the opposite baseline was Andre Agassi, thirty-five-years old, wearing his outfit of choice for that Open, a blue shirt and white shorts.

Lindsay Davenport and Elena Dementieva played a *long* match right before ours, so we didn't get on until about 10:00 PM But it didn't matter, because this was New York, and

Andre and I were the stars of the week, playing in the most hyped match of the tournament. Nobody was going anywhere. Not only were we two Americans playing in the quarters of our national slam, but we had become something that Americans can't get enough of: odds defiers. Andre was the oldest of the one hundred twenty-eight guys who had shown up to play in New York that year, and there he was among the final eight. And then there was my story, which, on the eve of the Open, had begun to be picked up not just by the tennis press, but also by the mainstream media. The sum total of our stories was a match where the stakes couldn't possibly have been higher.

I once had one of my best nights ever against Andre—that semifinal win in Washington, DC, back in 2002—and tonight seemed like it was going to be the same story. We came out into an atmosphere more suited to a football game than a tennis match, with twenty-three thousand people packed into the stadium. Because they had been waiting so long for our match to begin, it felt like every single one of them was pumped up— among them, of course, was the J-Block, enjoying the match from a prized vantage point: a coveted private suite.

When it's lit up, Ashe Stadium looks like a mammoth, octagonal mother ship getting ready to take off into the night, the lights casting the whole place in an otherworldly glow. This added to my sensation that the evening was the culmination of two and a half weeks straight out of a dream, and it had all gone by in a flash. I felt like one second I was about to play my first-round match in New Haven, then blinked and there I was standing across the net from Andre.

As good as the past few weeks had been, I was unprepared for the way the crowd took me in on this night. With questions of retirement swirling around him at all times, Andre was at a point in his career when he was the most beloved figure in tennis. *Anyone* who found himself competing against Agassi was automatically cast in the role of spoiler. But when we came out for our warm-up that night, the cheer that went up when my name was announced was just as big as the one that went up for Andre. As was the case at the Nadal match, there were blue J-Block shirts scattered throughout the stands, not just in the suite where my friends were sitting.

Though my mind was still struggling to comprehend all of this, my soul was ignited. I came out smoking and won the first two sets in about an hour, a bravura performance to the tune of that same chant, the "James! James! James!" that I heard even when my friends weren't actually screaming it. It was déjà vu all over again. Just as I had three years ago in Washington . . .

If you can win one set, you can win two.

. . . I had that player's high where I wasn't thinking, just flowing, swatting winners left and right, on the verge of a huge victory.

So if you can win one match, you can win two, right?

As I always did at times like these, I tried not to think about the context. On the changeover before the third set, I just focused on my friends, up in their box screaming and chanting their way right through the break, trying to will me across the finish line. My concentration held: I got ahead in the third set, as well, when I broke his serve, and within my sights was a kind of promised land, the semifinals of a major tournament, one match away from a slam final. I was already deeper into the draw than I had ever been at a major, and very close to going deeper still. I tried to focus on my friends, but I began to realize that I was on the brink of a career-making victory.

But as the play continued, the strangest thing started to happen—I felt the air go out of the crowd a little. As much support as I had had, nobody wanted to see Andre Agassi beaten in such quick fashion. More people started to pull for him. It was just enough of a shift to give me pause.

Don't think, James. Just play!

And that was all the opening a veteran like Andre needed to get something going. He reined in his game, and began going for more on his shots, and next thing I knew, he came back and won the third set.

If that had happened back in 2003, I'll tell you right now that I would've lost that match 6–1 in the fifth. But things had changed. I was disappointed that I'd dropped that set, but I had my wits about me. And, of course, I had my friends up there screaming down at me, letting me know that they believed in me. Their support was so palpable that I didn't let myself get down, not even when Andre won the fourth set, putting us even at two sets apiece.

Finally, early in the fifth set, perseverance paid off. I got ahead by breaking his serve, and at 5–4, I served for the match, but wouldn't you know it, Andre broke me. It was partially nerves on my part, and partially some outstanding returns on his, including two quality first-serves from me that he bludgeoned back my way with more pace than I could handle.

We both held our serves from 5-all and that's when the crowd went nuts, giving us a standing ovation.

"Game Blake. Six games all. Final set tie break."

I stood back from the service line and looked up. From the court of Ashe Stadium at night, it's difficult to focus on the crowd. You tend to look up, then farther up, then farther up, because you simply can't take it all in at once. I couldn't help but smile. I might have lost a two-set lead, and I might have failed to close out the match, but these were the moments I was craving during those months at home. I just basked in it for a few seconds before giving Andre a little nod that I was ready and stepping up into the court to receive serve. I won the first two points, then, on the third point, I moved him over to the side with a few high, looping forehands to his court, before smothering one down the line well out of his reach. I had a 3–0 lead, just four points away from the US Open semifinals.

When I swatted that last forehand, I felt like I was really meeting the moment, like I was witnessing in that shot what all my hard work had accomplished. There was only one person I thought of at times like that. I looked straight up into the sky over the stadium, and spoke right to my father: "I love you, Dad." Later, people told me that the words were captured by the television cameras, but it couldn't have been more intimate for me. I felt my father right there with me, felt his presence on the court the way it had been most of my life. I could hear his voice in my ear telling me to go for it, that all of my hard work this past year was for this moment right now.

I could also still hear the J-Block, trying so hard to will me forward to victory . . . "James! James! James!" . . . I wanted the win so bad, and I wanted it as much for them as I did for myself. I truly did. But Andre and I were locked in a true battle of wills, and accordingly, he stepped up. We traded a series of winners and errors, and a few minutes later we were all tied up at 4-all.

On the next point, just when I thought we were getting into a rally from the baseline, Andre smacked a backhand down the line that was so unexpected, all I could do was pray.

It was out by about two inches.

Thank God.

I admired Andre for going for that shot with so much on the line. At his age, he was possibly just a few points from going out of the US Open for the last time. Missing it put me up 5–4, and with two serves to go, all I had to do was win both of my points and that would be that. I'd be in the US Open semifinals.

Easier said than done, I stepped up to the line and hit a serve that bounced off the net cord and landed in. My next serve hit the cord and landed out. I served again and Andre stepped around it and absolutely crushed a crosscourt forehand that landed just past the service line and rocketed off the court. I looked up to the J-Block and could tell that they were feeling my pain. It was like Andre had just put the ball past all of us. But they didn't let the disappointment show for long; after a split second, they went right back to shaking their fists in the air and chanting my name and telling me that I could do it.

5-all.

Now it was my turn to go for broke: I served the next point. The rally was just getting started, when I stepped around my backhand and rocketed a forehand down the line. It was so close that my supporters in the crowd thought it was a winner and went nuts cheering for it. But I knew it was long, and the chair umpire confirmed it.

6–5 Andre. After my being up on him all night, he was the first one to reach match point. I couldn't believe it.

Do not back down, I told myself. *Go for your shots.*

On the next point, I went for the exact same shot again, stepping around another backhand and blasting a forehand right down the line. It made a perfect landing and skipped off the court, well out of his reach.

6-all.

We switched sides again, and on the next point we got into a long rally. He held his ground in the center of the court and ran me side to side. But I was the one really teeing off on the ball, thinking at least three times that he wouldn't get it back or that he'd land it short and I'd be able to get in and put it away for a winner. Somehow he kept scrambling around back there until he had the time to hit a drop shot. I scampered up and blocked it deep to his backhand, then leaned to my left to cover what I thought would be a crosscourt passing shot.

Andre went down the line and I didn't have a chance. The ball sailed right past me.

7–6. Another match point for Andre, this one on my serve.

My first serve landed out. I hit a safe second serve and he just knew it was coming. He stepped around it and walloped a forehand into the corner. It tattooed both lines and it was all over.

"Game. Set. Match. Agassi."

I could not believe it.

Andre and I shook hands and gave each other a hug at the net, then I went to the chair and threw a towel over my head while he soaked up the adulation and took his customary four-corner bow.

As I heard the crowd screaming for him, from the privacy of my towel, I relived the match in my head, the match I had held in my hand at more than one point, the match that had just gotten away from me. Was it really over? What had happened? A few hours ago, I couldn't believe I was going to win; now I couldn't believe that I had lost.

I looked down at the bracelet my father gave me, still around my wrist. I kissed it, and thought about how proud I thought he'd be of me, even though it didn't work out in the end. I thought about what he'd say to me at a moment like this: *You just keep working hard and you'll win the next time you're in a situation like that.*

Andre finished his bow, and the announcer did something they don't usually do: He announced my name, with great enthusiasm, "Ladies and gentlemen, James Blake!"

The crowd, including all my friends, gave me an ovation worthy of a winner. I stood and gave them a thumbs-up.

During his post-match interview, piped through the still-packed stadium over its PA system, Andre said, "I wasn't the winner tonight, tennis was."

I think he was right. I hear all the time from people who say that even though they aren't tennis fans, they were glued to their sets until one in the morning watching us battle it out that night. It really was a proud night for American tennis, and I was just happy to be a part of it.

But if I had played a part in that night, another big part was the fans, and in the end, that was really the great lesson of those amazing three weeks: I may be alone on the court, but I'm not alone in life. It's not whether I win a tennis match that counts, it's having people close to me that I know will make all the difference in the future, the same way it did in the past.

The J-Block which had started as a group of friends playing cards and eating chicken wings and burgers in my living room a year ago had become the thing that drove me to win, the energy that had pushed me to play the best tennis of my life. My hard work, my getting-better plan, my friends, and my family, these were the tools I used to get my life back, only now I had passed the point that I started at. I had entered unfamiliar territory and arrived there using my father as my guide. Now that I was on the other side of my past, I knew that as long as I continued to follow him, I was going to be all right.

EIGHT

GETTING BETTER

SEPTEMBER 2005– DECEMBER 2006

Never chase things . . . Let things happen.

—MICHAEL JORDAN, AS QUOTED IN
REBOUND *BY BOB GREENE*

"Please welcome, *Jaaaaames Blaaaaake.*"

It wasn't a stadium announcer this time. It was the goddess of daytime television, Oprah Winfrey. I was standing backstage in her Harpo Studios in Chicago, and when she called out my name, the production assistant at my side gave me a little nod and I walked out into the studio—a minimalist, dramatically lit set of steel and blue with the audience largely in the shadows— crossed a little bridge, and arrived on a platform where Oprah stood. In the center of this island was a yellow couch where we both had a seat.

Just before she summoned me to the stage, she played a video montage for the audience, one that swiftly summarized my career and my life, including photos of my father, and footage of the Agassi match.

I had done countless interviews before this one, but I had usually done them in sweaty tennis clothes on the court, or after a quick shower in the interview room, or maybe on the set of a sports show. A lot of people get into tennis for crossover moments like these, but I never sought them out. In 2002, *People Magazine* named me one of the sexiest men alive, and I didn't know how to react because I still felt like that skinny little kid with a back brace hidden under his shirt, and still had friends back home who teased him mercilessly about it.

Oprah talked to me about the Agassi match—it had become an overnight classic and catapulted me to a new level of fame—but we spent more time discussing my life off the court, all that stuff I went through in 2004. I was happy to recount it, but the attention was a bit overwhelming. A few weeks before appearing on *Oprah*, I had walked out onto the tundra-cold stage of the Ed Sullivan Theater in New York City and been interviewed by David Letterman. Because the US Open is aired on Letterman's network, CBS, the Open champion often makes an appearance the week after the tournament as part of his media victory lap. Not only had I not won the Open, but I had lost my quarterfinal match. And yet, there I was on the show, discussing it with Dave. Like Oprah would a few weeks later, he talked to me about my personal life as much as he did about the match and my career.

A few weeks later, the attention swelled to a whole new level when I was interviewed by legendary newsman Mike Wallace for a profile piece on *60 Minutes,* a show I'd always associated with world leaders and movie stars.

The line between my tennis and my life was disappearing, not just for me, but for fans as well.

As the story spread, I became aware that it meant something to people. There was a time, not that long ago, when strangers stopped me on the street for one reason: they were tennis fans. But starting in the fall of 2005, there was another reason: they had heard what I went through and how I overcame it. The interactions were different than they were pre-2004, when it was all about a quick handshake, my name scribbled on a tennis ball, a photograph. People wanted to tell me how my story had inspired them. Sometimes the inspiration was general, like a young person striving for a dream. Sometimes it was specific, like a sick person coping with an illness. Often the person who was inspired was decades older than I am, which humbled me.

Some of these interactions blew my mind—like the little girl who told me she had one of my interviews on her iPod and listened to it all the time for inspiration, or the family of a man who, in his sixties, careened headfirst into a net post and broke his neck. He wasn't as lucky as I was and was in intensive care, but his relatives reported to me that they told him my story to keep his spirits up.

Before 2004, the interactions ended as swiftly as they began: "Thanks, James, good to meet you. Bye."

Now the interactions were wrapping up more meaningfully: People wished me luck. They told me they were rooting for me. A lot of them even said, "Bless you." Our eyes would meet and I could tell that what I'd been through had meant something to them. This was an awesome thing to witness, and it made me wonder how many others might find something of value in my story, people who might be dealing with a rough patch of their own and weren't lucky enough to have something like a J-Block in their lives to help them out. This only strengthened my commitment to my game and to taking it as far as I could, because I wanted to show all the people who had tuned into my story just how far you can go if you just set your mind to it and don't give up.

In my career, I'd never felt an obligation to do more than perform my best on a tennis court, and be receptive to fans when I met them, but these interactions were causing me to rethink all of that. Though I had just gotten back on my feet, I felt compelled to do as much as I could to give something back to all these people with whom I was meeting and corresponding, and to the untold numbers of people who were out there pulling for me. I decided to focus on areas to which I felt the strongest personal connection and began looking for ways to funnel support to underprivileged kids, a nod to the Harlem Junior Tennis Program, and, for obvious reasons, to do my part to fight cancer.

One opportunity presented itself immediately. Thanks to the attention it received, and the T-shirts Nike produced for the US Open, the J-Block was becoming a worldwide phenomenon, and I realized that this gave me the power to do something. Carlos and I worked with Nike to set up a program whereby a full line of J-Block products (T-shirts, hats, wristbands, headbands, and so on) is sold at US Open Series tournaments, as well as stores and websites, with all the proceeds donated to the USTA Tennis and Education Foundation, which benefits public tennis and education programs throughout the country in an effort to grow the sport. (The Harlem Junior Tennis Program is funded partially by the USTEF, which I find especially gratifying.) In addition, Anne Worcester stepped up, donating a portion of the Pilot Pen proceeds to the New Haven Recreation Tennis Program as part of its J-Block promotions, helping to teach kids the same valuable lessons I learned up in Harlem as a little boy.

I also hooked up with Anthem Blue Cross and Blue Shield to create a benefit—Anthem LIVE!—to raise money for cancer prevention and research. This was a new experience for me, in which I wasn't just a player, but I also became a producer and promoter, calling on friends to help me in this cause. I was flattered that Andy Roddick accepted my invitation to play an exhibition match with me in the first-ever Anthem LIVE!, and that my childhood friend John Mayer, and another musician I know, Gavin DeGraw, came out to perform. We held the first event in early December of that year, and raised close to half a million dollars.

———

Back home for the holidays I engaged in all my usual late-December rituals, including assessing my game, and my prospects for the New Year. My first feeling this time was disbelief. Just a year earlier I had gone to bed on the eve of my departure for Australia, my left eye still not fully functioning, not knowing what to expect out of the year, out of the rest of my life, and now here I was, all the way back to where I had been before my wake-up call of a slump in 2003. In fact I was doing *better* than ever before: I had won two tournaments (following the US Open, I won an indoor event in Stockholm, Sweden) to the one I had notched in my entire *career* pre-2005; my ranking was at number twenty-three, compared to twenty-eight, where it had been at the end of 2002, not to mention compared to two hundred ten, where it had been that very April, just before I headed back to the minor leagues. If I took out all those months I had lost in 2004, and factored in the time it took to fully recover in the first half of 2005, I had actually lived out much of my vision for improvement in a relatively short time, a realization that made me believe, quickly, that I could still achieve everything I had wanted for myself before everything fell apart in 2004.

Talk about having positive *what-ifs;* going into December all I felt was upside. My motivation was greater than ever: I had come so close in that match against Andre. I had been up two sets and a break against one of the legends of the game, had been *two points* from victory in the fifth set, just inches from a slam semifinal. I was hungrier than ever to make every day count and really find that new level that I always believed I had in me.

So close, and yet so far. I put a good face on the Agassi loss in interviews, but the truth was that it hurt. A lot. There were points that I thought about at night, wondering what might have happened if I'd leaned right instead of left at 6-all in the tie break, when he passed me down the line, or if I'd taken a bit of a chance on a few second serves to keep him from teeing off on them.

This contemplation powered my off-seasoning training. In practice with Brian, or running drills with my brother and other players, I thought often about that match with Agassi. Pounding serve after serve, I remembered that match point, when he knew I was going to send him something he could hurt me on. I hit more serves than I could count, and did so every day, until I had strengthened not only my serve itself, but also my belief in it as something I could count on when I needed it most.

Ditto my backhand. Brian hit me backhand after backhand after backhand and ran me around all over the backcourt so I could continue to hone my defensive abilities, my patience, my willingness to wait for the right moment in each and every point I played. It was like December 2003 all over again: I was consumed with busting my butt to take things even further than before, only now, with my added realizations, namely that I wanted to succeed not just for myself, but also for my friends who were watching over me every step of the way, and for all of those people, the extended J-Block family, that I could just *feel* pulling for me everywhere I went.

All I perceived was promise. The media were talking me up like a top ten player. After my up-and-down start to the year, over the second half of the season I had won two tournaments, reached the final in another, and made it to the quarters of a slam for the first time.

All of the late-breaking success and attention of the year got to me during that December. After practice one day, sitting on the courtside bench and toweling off, I faltered for a moment and asked Brian if he thought that it was true, if he thought I was bound for bigger and better things than either of us had ever really thought were possible.

He looked at me incredulously. "I have no idea," he said.

Gotta love Brian. Even after all the excitement of the summer and fall, even after all the feel-good stories, he kept his eye on the ball. There was only one thing for us to focus on, as there always was. It was no different from when I was a petulant eleven-year-old, no different from when I was a rookie losing every week in Challenger events, no different from when I was down and out with half my face paralyzed, and no different from when we were getting ready to go back out on the road a year earlier.

Getting better was, and always would be, the goal. The rest would take care of itself, as it always did. I felt silly for asking the question.

But I was also full of excitement and optimism for what lay ahead. Of course, neither of us knew what fate might spring on us, but barring something totally unexpected, I felt sure that my greatest success lay just around the corner.

———

I had thought of myself as a man for a number of years, but embarking on 2006 I felt like more of a grown-up than I ever had before, like I was taking full responsibility for my talent and opportunity and was ready for whatever life might throw at me, on the court or off. That January I won a tournament in Sydney, Australia; on my way to the title, I beat world number six Nikolay Davydenko and former Australian Open finalist Arnaud Clement.

Talk about confidence building: I had won three titles in

my career, but the earliest in the year I had ever won one was August. To be in the first month of the season with a win under my belt changed my outlook for the entire year. Twelve months earlier, I hadn't won a title since 2002; now I had won three in the span of six months. I didn't do as well at the Australian Open as I might have liked, but my overall results in Australia pushed my world ranking into the top twenty by the end of January, another first for me.

Back in the States, in February, I made it to the final of the inaugural Tennis Channel Open in Las Vegas. My opponent there was Lleyton Hewitt. I had faced Lleyton six times before, and the meetings all had one thing in common: I had lost every time. But this time was different. This time, I won, 7–5, 2–6, 6–3, a score line of which I was especially proud because years earlier, had I dropped that second set, I likely would have lost belief and dropped the third as well. However, because the notion that if I won one set, I could win two was so ingrained in me, I had no reason to panic. I was so confident that I had all the tools, mentally and physically, to hang in there, that I actually never doubted that I *would* win.

The victory was another first in what was fast shaping up as a year of firsts. In March, I made it to my first Masters Series final in Indian Wells, California. My ranking was climbing higher and faster than ever, and on March 20, I cracked the top ten for the first time, weighing in at number nine.

In the weeks leading up to Wimbledon, I played Andy Roddick in the semifinals of Queens Club, a grass court tournament. Having never beaten Roddick in my career and never having had much success on grass, I was, by far, the underdog, especially since his game, with a monster serve that's most dangerous on grass, made him a natural on the surface. I beat him, putting me into yet another final that year, then, a few weeks later, I beat him in the final of Indianapolis, a hard-court tournament in the United States. My ranking climbed to number five. For the first time ever, I was the highest-ranking American tennis player in the world.

My profile was rising, too. In July, after years of discussion, I became the first-ever "celebrity ambassador" for Evian water.

As the tennis year turned a corner toward its final months, the US Open loomed large on the horizon. In keeping with my perennial goal of getting better, I didn't set any particular mark for myself, but I had a strong desire to perform at my absolute peak in New York, especially because, if there had been any unfinished business in my year, it was that I hadn't made it as deep into the slams as I'd have liked. Also, having played what had become widely considered one of the classic nighttime matches at the Open the prior year, I wanted badly to turn in a distinguished follow-up performance.

I got my wish. With the J-Block back in full force for all of my matches, I only dropped one set in my path through the first four rounds, taking me to US Open quarterfinals for the second consecutive year. Waiting for me there was world number one Roger Federer, widely considered a candidate for the mantle of "best player in history." Like so many of my peers, I had a losing record against Federer. We had played four times up to that point, and I hadn't managed to take a set off of him in any of our previous meetings. It was one of those situations for which the philosophy of getting better was born. I had done my best in all of our previous meetings, so I had a peace with myself, and I relished the challenge of continuing to improve against this particular foe until I persevered.

Not surprisingly, the powers that be scheduled Roger and me for a night session, and the crowd, while not as electric as the year before when I played Agassi in the same round, was still buzzing with excitement from the moment we played the first point. After a tantalizingly close first set, Roger had pulled ahead with the first two sets in his pocket and a lead in the third. But I dug in and broke his serve at a crucial moment, and we ended up playing a tie break, which I won, the first time I had taken a set from him and the first set that he had given up so far in the tournament.

He ended up winning the fourth set, and with it the match, but I had yet another example of how wise Brian's philosophy of getting better was: I had lost the match, but could honestly say that I had actually gotten better. I had finally won a set off of

Federer. And you know what they say: "If you can win one set, you can win two, and if you can win two sets . . ."

I left New York with a fire in my belly, eager for the next tournament and a chance to build on my good showing in New York. A few weeks later, I won another title in Bangkok, beating Marat Safin in the semifinals and world number three Ivan Ljubicic in the final, then the next week defended my title in Stockholm for my fifth tournament victory of the season, more than I'd won in my entire career before 2006.

Come the end of the tennis playing year, I had qualified for the Masters Cup, the most prestigious event on the men's professional tennis circuit, a year-end tournament for the top eight players of the year. (Although it doesn't strictly adhere to rankings; it's actually defined as the top seven players plus a player who's won a Grand Slam title and is in the top twenty.) Just getting into this event is a monumental achievement because it means you've had one of the best years of anyone in the world. To say that I had made the cut for the first time would be a massive understatement, because I hadn't even come close in previous years; I hadn't been among the top twenty at any point in my career before 2006.

My first two matches at the Masters Cup, against Nadal and Davydenko were full of high drama, but I won them both and qualified for the semifinals, where I met world number seven, David Nalbandian of Argentina, who had won the event the year before. By the time I got to the Nalbandian match, I felt on top of the world. Not only to be in Shanghai, but also to be toughing out all sorts of matches against some of the best players on Earth. I went for broke and played some of my best, most aggressive tennis of the year, advancing to the final by a score of 6–4, 6–1.

It was yet another first in this year of firsts: first time in the top twenty, first time in the top ten, first time in the top five, first year-end Masters Cup appearance, first seminal there, first *final* there. I had gotten so much better and done so much better than anyone could have expected. And all the while, I felt like all the things I had learned had come together to propel me to this moment: The lessons my father and Brian had instilled in me since childhood, reinforced and deepened by the events of the past two years, had all brought me to this point in my career, and my life.

Regardless of what happened in the final, just by getting there I had ensured that I would end the year with a ranking of number four in the world, and as the number one American, a great way to end my best year ever on tour.

As it turned out, I lost the final to Roger Federer. It would have been easy to be upset by the loss, and there was no question I was disappointed, but just getting to that final only furthered my belief that my brand of hard work and my outlook on my game was what had produced my success. To be one of the final two men standing in the last, most elite and selective tournament of the year was a triumph in itself.

———

There was no question that I had gotten better, better than I ever could have imagined, but there was still work to do, still new goals to be attained. A career, like a life, is a work in progress until it's over, and I was feeling pretty great—proud, even—about my progress of late. Having Roger out there could be a drag at times, but it gave me something to shoot for, another goal, right up there with winning a Grand Slam. Based on my results of the past year and a half, going all the way back to New Haven 2004, I had every reason to believe that it was all within my reach. I was playing the kind of sustained tennis, week in and week out, that makes you feel like it's only a matter of time before the next big milestone is attained, so long as you fulfill your end of the bargain, keeping your foot on the gas and continuing to push yourself as hard as possible to make it happen.

Simply put, I headed home from Shanghai as successful as I'd ever been, and as hungry for *more* success as I'd ever been.

A few weeks later, *Sports Illustrated* published a feature piece about me. In it, the magazine's tennis writer called me the "face of American tennis" and one of the "hottest players" in the sport. I didn't even ask Brian what he thought about those sentiments and whether he expected me to live up to them, because I already knew what he'd say—"I have no idea."—and he'd have been right, of course.

But I felt like I'd be able to live up to it. You can't know for sure until you get out there and prove it, but then, more than ever, I felt like I could.

I could hardly wait for the new season to begin.

EPILOGUE
HOME FOR THE HOLIDAYS

It's November, but you wouldn't know it from the weather. I'm back in Tampa and it's eighty-something degrees outside. I'm just home from Shanghai and I'm in the backseat of a car coming home from the airport.

In my jetlagged state, the whole year really does feel like a dream. My whole life feels like a dream—now more than ever. I get to my house and turn in for the night. The next day, I get a call from Becky Stoltz, Carlos's assistant at IMG.

"Oh, great, you're back," she says. "I have piles of mail for you. I'll send them on down."

I take the next two weeks off. I need to. I've never played so many matches in a year, and my year has never run so late. Evan and some of the guys from Fairfield come down to visit and we hang out, play golf, poker, and whatever. It's like old times.

Somewhere in there I come home to find that a pile of enormous padded bags has shown up from IMG. They're crammed with letters and postcards. I don't need to open them to know that they are not only from tennis fans, because, just as my personal interaction with fans has changed a lot in the past two years, so have the cards and letters: they're full of hopes and dreams. Some put a smile on my face and some break my heart. I answer what I can, but the truth is that I can't answer most of them. Not in the way they deserve to be answered. I guess I could hire somebody to answer them for me, but I think that would be worse than not writing back. I hope that the people who write to me know that I got their letters. I hope they know that it means the world to me. I hope they understand why they don't hear from me.

The letters also whet my appetite for the fan interaction I'll have in the coming weeks. While it's the off-season for us tennis players, it's also a mini-season unto itself. Call it the Benefit Season. In the next two weeks, I'll play exhibition matches at Andre's benefit in Richmond, Virginia; Mardy Fish's in Vero Beach, Florida; and attend Andy Roddick's charity dinner in Austin. I'll also play some exhibitions in Texas, where a portion of the proceeds will benefit the USTA.

It's December 7, 2006, and I'm standing on a tennis court at Old Dominion University in Norfolk, Virginia, that has been set up for a one-night-occasion—Anthem LIVE!—the sophomore edition of last year's cancer benefit.

There's a buzz in Norfolk because Andre Agassi has graciously accepted my invitation to play an exhibition with me, which will be the centerpiece of the evening. There will also be a brief performance by Boyd Tinsley of the Dave Matthews Band, and doubles between myself and Thomas and Bob and Mike Bryan, whose father Wayne is the MC for the evening. Just as it was last year, putting this event together has been humbling: I'm blown away that all of these talented people have come to help support a cause that's so near and dear to my heart, and especially moved that Andre, who had just retired, showed up for me.

Andre has warmed up with a local college player, but he wants to warm up some more. He and I come out on the court and begin to hit. Andre hasn't played a competitive match since he retired after going out in the third round of the US Open on Labor Day. But he's still in awesome shape, and we begin to rally, hitting the ball back and forth.

As is so often the case, being on a court, playing tennis, brings back memories. I think about how I felt all those years ago when I was fresh out of college and serving as sparring partner to Sampras, Courier, and Martin in the suburbs of Boston. I still feel a little like that hitting with a legend like Andre.

We begin to pick up the pace. He may have limped out of

the US Open with a creaky back, but now that he isn't punishing his body on a daily basis, he's hitting the ball like old times. It's forehand to forehand now. There's only about twenty or so people in the entire auditorium, but he and I are in our own little world.

I strike the ball. I think of my father, about how we're all really here for him. The foundation at Memorial Sloan-Kettering Cancer Center, to which some of the money raised tonight will go, bears his name.

Andre hits it back to me. I think of my mother, hanging out in a makeshift locker room just out of my sight, with Bob and Mike Bryan. She seems to be having a good time, but I know the subject of the benefit isn't easy for her.

I whack it again. I think of that match Andre and I played at the Open. It still stings, more than a year later, that I lost, but what a thrill it was to be a part of it. What a thrill it will be to play against him tonight, probably for the last time, even though it's just an exhibition.

I pull Andre out wide and he runs over there—making that patented Andre exertion sound, like a guy benching three hundred pounds—plants himself and crushes a forehand to my side of the court, just past the service line and right on the sideline.

I look up at him and he has a huge smile on his face.

"If I'd known I'd enjoy playing this much, I would've retired a long time ago," he says.

He's called up yet another memory for me: "Isn't it great, I say," thinking about all those weeks I spent holed up with zoster, wondering if I'd ever play another professional match. "When you've been away, even just to hit balls is so much fun."

He just smiles. The acoustics in this place are a little weird, and I think maybe he didn't quite hear me, or just didn't realize what I was referring to. But the unpleasantness of that year comes flooding back, and as I send another ball his way, I remember for the thousandth time how lucky I am to even be standing here.

The night is a rousing success. Combined with last year's event, we've already raised over a million dollars. I tell the crowd that I'll be back next year.

The next day, I get in a car with a rep from IMG and the local public relations agent for Anthem Blue Cross and Blue Shield, and we drive out to nearby Newport News, to a not-for-profit inner-city tennis program called Achievable Dreams Academy, where they use tennis as a tool to educate underprivileged kids. I visit with the kids and I find myself thinking of my time at the Harlem Junior Tennis program. Arthur Ashe once visited us there. I'm too young to really remember, but my mom does. My agent, Carlos, met him once too, in his hometown of Cleveland, and still has the picture to prove it. These moments mean something to kids. I answer a slew of questions, about everything from what my favorite match was to how I came back, then get in the backseat of a car with a driver I've never met and start the two-hour drive to Richmond, where Andre's event begins in a few hours.

———————

Appropriately enough, my last benefit of the year, on December 22, is for the Harlem Junior Tennis Program, right back at the Armory. The place is unrecognizable from the days when I used to play there. It's undergone a multi-million-dollar renovation. With all the indoor courts that have closed in Manhattan in recent years, it's probably the nicest facility in town.

John and Patrick McEnroe show up to play that night. So does my brother. Jim Courier is there, and so is former New York City mayor David Dinkins, who's a huge tennis fan. We all play, then I hop a plane back to Tampa to hook up with some friends who are already there, waiting to squeeze some more precious time together out of my weeks off.

With that done I head home. Back to Fairfield for Christmas.

There's a lot that hasn't changed: I still own the same house. I still have some of the same roommates I've had for years. Most of my friends who have lived in town since high school are still here. I still have the same December punctuated by my rotating series of *what-ifs.*

But a few things *have* changed. It's still hard with my father gone. Nothing's been the same without him. We don't talk about him much, my mother and Thomas and I, but we all think about him. For me that means continuing to live by his lessons every day, continuing to work hard and to solve whatever problems confront me. I'll never stop trying to honor his memory and to squeeze as much as I can out of my talent, to pay tribute to all the belief he had in me.

I'm also going to keep operating on the wisdom that Brian has instilled in me since I was a tantrum-throwing little boy, by keeping the focus on getting better, and by drawing on my life off the court to fuel my success on the court. I'm going to keep my friends and family foremost in my mind and heart, even if most of my time is spent elsewhere, keeping in touch by e-mail.

And, in the back of my mind, I'm going to remember that unforeseen events might alter the course of my life at any time— who knows what net posts might be lurking up ahead? If something bad happens, I'll get through it the best I can. In the meantime, I'm going to keep treating my career, and my life, like a sprint, not a marathon, and make the most out of each and every opportunity.

At the very least, I'm going to go to bed each night knowing I did the best I could to get better, and that I did everything possible to earn the attention that so many people—friends and family, intimates and strangers—have lavished upon me over the years.

That's what I'm going to do.

Every day.

That much I'm sure of.

GLOSSARY

If you don't play or watch tennis, you might find these definitions of certain terms used throughout the book helpful.

ACE: A serve that the returner doesn't even get a racket on. Not to be confused with a *service winner*, which is a serve that the returner hits, but either puts in the net or outside the lines.

AD COURT: The left side of a player's side of the court, the side where he or she would be standing to receive serve should the score reach "ad"

APPROACH SHOT: A shot behind which a player will come to the net in hopes of putting away a volley

CHANGEOVER: The switching of sides that takes place every other game in a tennis match, and after every six points in a tie break

DEUCE COURT: The right side of a player's side of the court, the side where he or she would be standing to receive serve should the score reach "deuce"

DROP SHOT: A shot hit just over the net that, thanks to spin or lack of force, bounces short

GROUND STROKES: Shots hit after a bounce, or off the ground, namely forehands and backhands. Most shots hit in tennis are ground strokes.

LINES: The baseline is the line that defines the back of the court on both sides. Sidelines define the boundaries for singles and doubles play. The space between the singles and doubles sidelines is called the *alley*. The line that runs from the net into the court is the center service line, and the line that runs perpendicular to it is the service line. When serving, the server must place the ball into the box formed by the center service line, the singles sideline, and the service line.

LOB: A high, looping shot usually employed to go over, rather than around, an opponent who has come to the net. A *topspin lob* is hit with enough spin that the ball comes down more quickly and accelerates when it bounces, turning this defensive shot into an offensive one.

RALLY: An exchange of shots from the baseline

RETURN, OR SERVICE RETURN: The second shot of any point; the first shot hit back by the player receiving serve

SCORING: A tennis match comprises points, games, and sets. The first player to win four points wins a game. You start at Love, which means "zero." The points are scored 15, 30, 40, game. If both players reach 40, the score is called deuce, and a player must win two consecutive points to earn the game. The point after deuce is called either ad-in (the server's advantage) or ad-out (the receiver's advantage). You win a set by getting to six games, with a margin of at least two games, before your opponent (you can also win by a score of 7–5). If you get to six games all, you generally play a tie break, scored with "regular" numbers (0, 1, 2, 3, etc.) until one player reaches a score of seven (again, by a margin of two points), alternating serve after the first point, and then after every two points. Matches comprise sets and are either best of three or best of five.

SERVE: The shot that begins the point. The server is allowed two serves. If he or she misses the first, it's called a *fault*. If the second serve is unsuccessful, it's a *double fault*, and the point goes to the receiver.

THE TAPE: The very top of the net, as in "My shot hit the tape and landed back on my side of the net"

UNFORCED ERROR: An avoidable miss, made when a player should have been able to keep the ball in play with relative ease

VOLLEY: A shot, most often executed near the net, that takes the ball before the bounce and traditionally doesn't involve a swing but rather a firm wrist and a blocking of the ball by the racket. Recent generations of players have added the *swinging volley,* which is essentially a groundstroke taken out of the air. A *half-volley* is a nonswinging blocking of the ball after it's bounced.

WILDCARD: Direct entry into the main draw of a tournament, granted to players whose ranking would otherwise require them to win three rounds of *qualifying* matches in order to compete

WINNER: A shot that bounces in the court and which your opponent does not get a racket on, earning you the point

ACKNOWLEDGMENTS

First of all, I have to thank my family: Mom, Thomas, Chris, Howard, and, of course, Dad. We might not be most people's idea of America's "normal" family, but I think we all know how great we have it. Being the baby of the family, I have nothing but wonderful role models to look up to.

I also have to thank my friends, those who were around for me in my many good times and even more importantly, the friends who were around during the tough times. Evan, Daly, Laura, Sara, Caraly, J.P., Kim—you guys made me smile on the inside before I was able to on the outside. My Mather 401 crew is never forgotten. You guys were such a big part of who I am because of the time in my life you were so close to me, and that will keep you close to me forever. Stak, Grady, R.D., Lucas, Stapher, Walshy, Carfagns, Shinners, Verdini. I have no idea how that random selection goes, but I won the lottery to live with you guys. All of the guys on tour have meant a great deal to me, especially Mardy, Andy, Robby, Taylor, Bob and Mike, Goldie, Todd, Kelly, Scott, and Bo—we may be sometime-competitors, but we will always be friends. That means a lot to me and it helped me to get back on tour knowing that I'd be coming back to friendly faces in the locker room. Andre, thank you for playing the way you did against me. You taught me a lot on the court, but I learn even more seeing you as a father and husband. The amount of care you put into your relationships off the court is admirable, and that's why, even if you never play tennis again, I and so many others will still look up to you as a role model.

A very special thank you to my coach-mentor-friend Brian Barker. I can't think of words to express how much you have put up with. I am continually amazed at how you have kept my spirits high for the last sixteen years, without fail, in every single situation. I'm not sure anyone else could have had me laughing in a hospital room with a broken neck and clay and sweat all over me. Mark Merklein, you have been a doubles partner, a friend, and now a trainer. The friend part has been the most important. I have learned the most from that aspect of our relationship. There aren't many people in the world with a bigger heart than yours. Carlos Fleming, I could thank you for all the deals you have done for me, or the money that you have put in my pocket, but if it came down to it, I'd spend all of that money to keep your friendship. I have been thankful for the decision I made at the beginning of my career. It is so amazing to know that I have an honest friend that can represent me with the dignity you have. Kevin O'Connor at Saddlebrook has taken me under his wing since I was a clueless kid just leaving home for the first time. From picking out my house to picking out my furniture, you have helped me in so many ways beyond the tennis court. You are the main reason that Tampa ever feels like home to me and my brother. PMac, thanks for having me around the Davis Cup team. Being there in South Carolina wasn't very helpful to the team, but it meant a lot to me because it gave me the inspiration to be a part of that again. Thank you for having confidence in me time and time again. We will get that cup home to the States one of these days.

I have to thank all of the people directly responsible for putting this book together and getting it into your hands. First of all, my collaborator, Andrew Friedman, has been excited about this project since Day One. It made my job so much easier to have an experienced writer to show me the ropes, especially one who had an honest appreciation for the whole story. Thanks also to our editor, Matt Harper, for his attention to detail, enthusiasm, and good ideas, to Laurye Blackford for acquiring the book in the first place, to the rest of the team at HarperCollins for their interest in my story and for putting together a great project, and to Lisa Queen, who agents books for IMG. (I again need to thank Carlos Fleming, as well as his assistant, Becky Stoltz, for putting me in contact with Lisa to start this whole ball rolling, just another reason I'm so glad and proud to be a part of the IMG family.) Matt Van Tuinen, I have always enjoyed working with you at the Pilot Pen, and I appreciate all your great work getting the word out about this book. Everyone who was interviewed for this book was inconvenienced on my behalf, and most of you guys know how much I hate inconveniencing you, so I have to thank all of you again: Mom, Thomas, Brian, Laura, Evan, Daly, Bobby D., Mardy (Tobes and Samuel Duvall for setting that up), Neps (Kelly Wolf and Tom Ross for setting that up), Carlos, Pat McEnroe, John Honey, and Anne Worcester.

I wouldn't be sharing this story at all if not for the doctors who have helped in this process. I can't thank you enough for that. Dr. Lutz at The Hospital for Special Surgery: I'm sorry you had to see an injury like mine that wasn't a car accident, but totally self-inflicted; you did a great job in improvising with a stubborn kid like me. Dr. John Kveton and Dr. Mark Bianchi helped out so much with the zoster. Dr. Bianchi, your personal care may have saved my career; I have no idea what I would have done that Saturday morning if I didn't have your cell number and you hadn't made sure I got to the emergency room. Dr. Kveton, your knowledge and candor were so helpful in taking the pressure off during a year about which I was too stressed out. Additionally,

Dr. Richard Weininger has been helpful with many medical questions; thank you for your availability.

Thank you to Chris Griffin for running my website and putting so much of yourself into it. You always keep me on my toes and up-to-date on the things that I need to know in this world. You also make it possible for my fans to keep up-to-date on what I've been doing. And thanks to each and every one of those fans who visit my website, watch me play in person or on TV, or is an official member of the J-Block. Those original J-Blockers have a special place in my heart, too: Andy J., Bobby D., Bobby C., Haus, Pass, Emily, Christiana, Paco, Kristie, Romer, Davis, Portlock. It means so much to me, to see you up there screaming.

Thanks to Nike for having faith in me. Mike Nakajima, Bruce Schilling, Roy Sakaguchi, Aaron Rapf, Suzanne Pond, Monica Kolstad, Ricky Roundtree: you guys said when I signed with Nike that we would be a family and it has been true the whole time. To know that you guys stuck with me in the hard times made me want to make it worthwhile when I got back to full strength. I wish there was some way I could repay all of you for the hard work and dedication you've shown. I am also very proud to have an association with Anthem Blue Cross and Blue Shield and especially with Tom Byrd and Keith McMullin there. We have raised over one million dollars for cancer research, and I hope we can continue on the same path. Thanks also to the people at Evian for making me feel welcome as well; I am proud to be associated with you. Finally, to Richard Presser of Hugo Boss, you have helped me look good in any situation. Thanks for all the times you have been a fan, and thanks for putting the clothes on my back.

I know I am supposed to be contemptuous of the media, since I'm an athlete, but it's just not true in my case. The media have been great to me, and I want to thank them all for doing their job with diligence.

Thanks also to Alvaro, Katie H. (thank you for taking care of me), Nish, Rene, the USTA, Terry London, Craig, Dan, Hogan, Al, Kev, Pete and Bridgette S., Jill Smoller, Camila Knowles, Erica Fisk, Erica Muhlemann, Jay Kramer, Claudia Butzky, Keenan Minogue, Rachel Nelson, and Jon Nee. Mats Wilander, thanks for believing in me; just the thought that a player of your caliber thought that I had a chance to make it in the pros when I met you helped my dream become a reality.

Thanks to all the kids I have come in contact with at the Harlem Junior Tennis Program and the Shriners Hospital for Crippled Children. I was a part of both of them growing up and now hope that more doors are opened to all the people who are involved with both places. Good luck to all of you. I also have to thank Kirsten Peterson and her two daughters, Ava and Emily, just for being who they are. Ava and Emily might be many years younger than I, but they are an inspiration and always will be. Don't ever lose that joyous spirit that the whole family possesses.

As I look over this list, I can't believe how many people have touched my life in so many ways. No wonder I made the comeback I did. Thank you all!